Works by *John P.*

Biographical Novels

The Fourteenth State (Ethan Allen)
Triumph of the Swan (Richard Wagner and King Ludwig II of Bavaria)

Historical Novel

Mt. Soledad Love Story

Biographical Screenplays

Degas (Edgar Degas and the Impressionist Revolution in Art)
The Mighty Kuchka (Nikolai Rimsky-Korsakov and the Russian Five)

Inspirational / Motivational

Around the World in a Wheelchair

Treatments and Screenplays

Inquiring Minds (Teens challenge education system)
California (Father Junipero Serra to Stathood)
Mt. Soledad Love Story (film version available to producers)
Serial Monogamy (A quest for success happiness and love)

Website

www.jproach.org   (contains a sample chapter of each book and color photos to support books)

AROUND THE WORLD IN A WHEEL CHAIR

A Motivational Adventure For the Disabled

by
John P. Roach Jr.

authorHOUSE®

AuthorHouse™
1663 Liberty Drive, Suite 200
Bloomington, IN 47403
www.authorhouse.com
Phone: 1-800-839-8640

First published by AuthorHouse 11/30/2007

ISBN: 978-1-4343-4142-6 (sc)
ISBN: 978-1-4343-4143-3 (hc)

Printed in the United States of America
Bloomington, Indiana

This book is printed on acid-free paper.

DEDICATION

This book is dedicated to Deborah J Johnson

Contents

PREFACE

This book is a true story about a beautiful brave woman with a serious disability affecting her balance and mobility that became determined to not let her recently discovered Disability change her goals or the course and direction of her life,

CHAPTER I

THE PLAN

Debbie and I met in Burlington, Vermont in 1989, she was the manager of one of Burlington's most fashionable woman's store and I owned my own business in Burlington and had previously opened a branch office in La Jolla, CA where I planned to eventually move. A year later we both moved to La Jolla where we lived on the oceanfront. Our vacations from La Jolla typically were enjoyed visiting the western states from La Jolla by car.

It was in September of 1993, that Debbie and I took our first cruise together. The Cunard ship HMS Sagafjord, bound from Los Angeles, CA through the Panama Canal to Ft. Lauderdale FL with ports of call in Mexico, Costa Rica and Aruba.

CARIBBEAN SEA

Both of us have cruised before mostly in the Caribbean with the longest cruise of only a week and typically seven islands in seven days. This Sagafjord Cruise however, was a month in duration as we continued again on the Sagafjord from Ft. Lauderdale to Rio de Janeiro, Brazil. The most memorable highlights of our 1993 cruise were both the interesting transit of the Panama Canal and the extra days we spent in Rio de Janeiro.

Now that both of us have our sea legs for extended cruises we defined our ultimate goal for adventure as a world cruise. We researched World Cruises and found them to be about 100 days in length mostly commencing in January and heading South of the Equator where it is warm and by the time they finally reach Europe they typically schedule very few ports of call before heading back to the United States. We both decided we would prefer to see Europe as a Grand Tour before we embarked on a world cruise.

So our goals become more focused, the order in which we shall seek adventure became apparent.

First: The Fifty States, including many National Parks and Historic Sites.

Second: Europe

Third: A World Cruise

Each year we planned an interesting vacation that would have the cumulative effect of adventure and seeing the world and meeting the people and learning of and respecting their culture. Our emphasis was to make sure we visited what is close to home right here in the United States, before taking on the world. Previously I spent ten days in Alaska visiting sites as far North as Point Barrow and another week in Hawaii as well as a cross-country trip with my son by car, so it seemed only logical that we concentrate on visiting those few states that remain of the 50 states, before we resumed our exploration of foreign countries.

With all these vacation plans, disaster strikes in the year 2000. While at a cocktail party in San Diego, someone intentionally slipped drugs into Debbie's glass of wine. She became dizzy and said let's go home. We looked for her purse and it was not found. The tennis bracelet I bought for her in Brazil was also gone. I immediately took her the few blocks to home. In her dressing room she took off one high heel shoe and when trying to take off the other fell backwards and cracked her skull on the door jam. Blood was everywhere, I wanted to call 911, and she said no and wrapped her head in a towel to stop the bleeding. The dressing room was covered with blood and finally the bleeding stopped.

The next morning she awoke with two black eyes caused by the severity of the blow to the back of her head. Eventually the black eyes went away and she seemed to be fully recovered. We later found that six other women were drugged that same evening, one in a coma for many weeks before she recovered. Still others had their jewelry stolen.

Tragic symptoms started to appear two years later, at first it was difficulty in walking, then her inability to step off a curb. Countless doctor appointments, MRI and brain scans yielded a confirmation of severe brain and nerve damage due to her fall two years ago.

CHAPTER II

THE FIFTY STATES

At first Debbie used a cane then a walker and finally a wheelchair. She was quite brave during these years and accepted her worsening condition. Determined not to let her disability change our lifestyle we tried to evaluate the changes put before us.

During these same years we often received comps at five star hotels in Las Vegas, Laughlin and San Diego. We had so many free rooms that sometimes we were able to get away for a month at a time. Las Vegas, Laughlin, Lake Tahoe and Phoenix are so near many National Parks that we would often combine visiting the National Parks during the day with overnight stays at luxury hotels.

Our preferred mode of travel was by car, we found the airplane since 911 to be the least acceptable form of travel for anyone, not just the disabled. Airline travel has degenerated to such an unacceptable level, that we fly only as a last resort. The automobile, train and ship can provide the kind of humane comfort that air travel once had, but have since discarded.

In 2001 we toured the deep South by car. Biloxi, Mississippi, to New Orleans and on to Arkansas and the many historic sites and National

Parks and Monuments along the way. Of special interest to Debbie was Hot Springs National Park, Arkansas; where wheelchair ridden President Roosevelt often visited. FDR, like Debbie was not about to let his disability hold him back.

We continued on to Tennessee, Missouri and Oklahoma, three more states we have never previously visited. We ordered the famous ribs at the Piedmont in Memphis, walked along Beale Street and asked our pal Duncan in Oklahoma if he could make to same style ribs on his outdoor barbeque, and of course he did.

With only three states to go to complete the fifty we scheduled them for a 2002 vacation as they are far from San Diego or Vermont where we lived previously. If you had to guess the three remaining states, you would probably be right in guessing North Dakota, South Dakota and Nebraska.

We visited Theodore Roosevelt National Park, commemorating the environmentalist who set aside so much parklands in the United States and then on to Mt. Rushmore and South Dakota's National Parks.

Nebraska, a most central state in our country holds for us a special meaning as it completes our mission of a visit to all fifty states. Agate National Monument exceeded our expectations as it holds further evidence of cataclysmic events that shaped our world.

When we arrived at Scott's Bluff National Monument, the docent stayed after hours to explain the significance to us of the pioneers Calistoga wagons crossing the Great Plains looking for the bluff to guide them to the Oregon Trail on the route to the West,

Brave Deborah, never let her disability even slow us down with completing the fifty states. So much time was spent outdoors, in so many National Parks, admiring nature and smelling the roses and living life to the fullest.

"How about Europe Debbie, are you ready?"

"No, next year let's go to Vermont to visit family, then Banff National Park and Lake Louise, in Alberta, Canada; and then maybe Europe."

CHAPTER III

PLANNING A EUROPE TRIP

Europe is now in the plan and soon we hope. Each year I would create an itinerary for a Europe trip that we would put on hold for a more practical time. We desired to see family in Vermont prior to such a trip and also visit to Banff National Park and Lake Louise in Alberta, Canada before venturing to Europe.

2003 Vermont Trip.

Other than my son and his wife who at that time lived in San Diego County my family and Debbie's family both live in Vermont, so in 2003 Vermont it is scheduled before Europe. This I am sure you realize for practical purposed involves the dreaded airplane. Airlines are pretty good about attending to wheelchair-ridden flyers, but it ends there. Did you ever notice that couples come in two's and the seats on airlines are in three's?

You choose a window and aisle seat knowing full well a stranger will be seating between each couple. Larger aircraft have seats five and six across, we once flew from Los Angeles to Tahiti in middle seats. You never want to relive this terrible experience. Blame the engineers who design these flying profit-centers. The flight from San Diego, to

Detroit and on to Burlington VT was uneventful. The return flight had a five-hour equipment delay in Detroit. The visit to family was certainly a fun visit. And we decided that the next visit will be by ship to New York on our return from our proposed Europe trip.

2004 Banff National Park, Alberta, Canada

Ahh! Back to the open roads by car driving from San Diego to Grand Teton and Yellowstone National Parks and on to the Canadian Border between Montana and. Alberta.

The Border Guard approaches our car and I roll down the window.

"Passports please?"

"We both have passports but we left them home."

Why didn't you bring them?

We used to live in Vermont and go to Montreal on weekends and never needed a passport."

"Where are going?"

"Banff National Park and Lake Louise."

"Where are you from now?"

"San Diego, California."

"Would you go to Switzerland without a passport?"

"No."

"Why not?"

"They require one."

"So does Canada!"

"Since 9 – 11?'

"Yes!"

"You are very far from home, so I will let you go, but next time, bring your passport."

As we leave the boarder and enter Alberta heading for Calgary Debbie says:

"What a coincidence that the emergency number 911 and date 9-11 are the same number."

"Wow Deb, I never thought of that."

This trip was very worthwhile, we stayed overnight in Calgary, entered Banff in morning, had breakfast at Banff Springs Hotel and enjoyed Banff National Park on our way to Lake Louise, which is one of the most beautiful sights in North America, and is absolutely breath taking.

2005 HIGH DESERT VACATION

2005 Santa Fe, New Mexico.

My son and daughter-in-law surprised us by selling their California home and moving, to Santa Fe, NM, so a Europe trip will have to wait still another year while we plan a high desert vacation in Arizona, New Mexico and Nevada where we will visit some National Parks while staying at nearby Resorts where we receive comp's for free nights in Laughlin, NV, Phoenix, AZ and Las Vegas.

2006 San Diego, California.

Five years of planned itineraries that never came to fruition, we decided in 2006 that now is the time as Debbie's health has continued to deteriorate to the point where we think she could still travel with the aid of a wheelchair. Around our home Debbie walks holding on to furniture or touching the walls when necessary. Occasionally, she will have a good day and can walk around not touching anything for support.

We planned to stay four months on this trip with the preferred mode of travel to be by ship or automobile with aircraft flights kept to a minimum and used only as a last resort. In theory we wanted at least 6 weeks on land in Europe to explore places where ships can not go and the remainder of the trip to be by the most comfortable form of travel, the cruise ship. Booking six different cruises would allow us to enjoy Europe's ports combined with a car rental for six weeks to allow us the flexibility to see the interior.

CHAPTER IV

TRANSATLANTIC VOYAGE GALVESTON, TEXAS TO ROME, ITALY CELEBRITY M/V GALAXY

We boarded the Celebrity ship Galaxy in Galveston, Texas for a 16 day crossing of the North Atlantic Ocean bound for Rome, Italy. Neither of us has been on a ship since 1993 when we did both a Panama Canal Cruise and a Brazil Cruise and we both had needless concerns about a sixteen-day Atlantic crossing. This cruise became a wonderful experience regarding wheelchair accessibility, the exquisite food, friendly caring staff and pleasant passengers. After a few days we gained the confidence that crossing the Atlantic would be a great experience.

The ports of call were Key West, FL, Nassau, that we previously visited then Punta Delgado, Azores, Lisbon, Portugal; Palma de Mallorca, Spain and Rome, Italy.

PORTUGAL

Azores.

Our first landfall across the Atlantic was the Azores Islands a possession of Portugal. We docked at the port of Punta Delgado on the island of St. Michael. We were quite surprised about the beauty of this island with its very green mountains and houses with red tile roofs.

In the Azores I pushed her wheelchair along the quay, and we did bars and restaurants and had conversations with the locals. Debbie was still a little hesitant about having her photo taken with the wheelchair. I would sit her at a table, remove the wheelchair and take her picture.

The waterfront has beautiful walkways made with small mosaic tiles similar to what impressed us so much in Rio de Janeiro, in Brazil.

Lisbon.

An earthquake destroyed Lisbon in 1755 and the city was rebuilt to withstand quakes, so Lisbon is quite modern. Entering the harbor our ship goes under the 25th of April Bridge commemorating Portugal's revolution to a democracy. The bridge was built by US Steel who also built the Golden Gate Bridge, thus the similarity.

The Monument of the Discoveries honors Henry the Navigator and other Portuguese explorers. Most impressive is the Statue of Christ with arms outstretched overlooking Lisbon and its harbor. It is a copy of Christ the Redeemer welcoming visitors to Rio de Janeiro.

Fatima.

One hundred and fifty miles north of Lisbon is the religious shrine of Fatima. From Lisbon we traveled to Fatima, Portugal, where saw the shrine where the apparition took place and spent the entire day. Both

Lisbon and Fatima are wheelchair friendly destinations, although the cathedral at Fatima is not. I did prey at Fatima for Debbie's recovery.

In Fatima, we visited the exact spot where the Virgin appeared in a bush before the three children in 1917. The two cousins died years ago but Lucy died less than a year before our visit. The shrine is large and commemorates the 70,000 witnesses to the Miracle of Fatima. Each year on May 13 and October 13 more than 100,000 pilgrims visit Fatima and pay homage to the Miracle.

We enjoyed the scenery to and from Fatima as quite interesting passing through olive groves, vineyards and pretty countryside. Under construction is a four lane divided highway from Lisbon to Fatima with about half the distance already completed.

BALLERIC ISLANDS

These three Mediterranean islands have changed hands so many times that they finally belong to Spain.

Mallorca.

One day as a young man while working at IBM Headquarters in Armonk, NY, I was surprised when the elevator the door opened and Thomas J. Watson Jr. the IBM Chairman entered while conversing with an associate. The associate asked about the Chairman's vacation and Tom related his experiences in Mallorca. The door opened and they left the elevator and left me with dreams of someday visiting this beautiful island.

Well as we approach the island, it appears a mountainous jewel with beautiful beaches and many luxury hotels. We docked at the capital city of Palma de Mallorca; I had two objectives on this one-day visit. I was already experiencing the enthusiasm of the IBM Chairman and secondly to complete research on my forthcoming book on California.

We hired a cab for the entire day to visit the tiny town of Petra, some 60 miles inland of Palma de Mallorca. Petra is the humble birthplace of Fr. Junipero Serra, the Father of California and one of California most honored citizens. Each State in the United States is permitted two statues of their hero's in the National Statuary Hall below the rotunda of the capitol building in Washington, DC. California's statues are Fr. Junipero Serra and Ronald Regan. A statue of Kit Carson, representing New Mexico brings to mind his heroism in early California History as well and he is an important character in my forthcoming book on California. Incidentally, I am the author of the biographical novel of Ethan Allen titled, *The Fourteenth State.* Representing Vermont in the National Statuary Hall below the rotunda of the capitol building is a statue of Ethan Allen.

Once in Petra we found the home of Fr. Junipero Serra that was a tiny home made of stone. The small walled-in back yard had an outdoor oven and grill, and a small hut for animals.

Within a half a block from the Serra home is the Fr. Serra Museum containing many artifacts and memorabilia from his career of building missions throughout Mexico, the Baja and up the California Coast from San Diego to Sonoma one horseback day ride from each other to protect travelers from the wild?

Our bi-lingual cab driver translated the words of the curator of the museum who was extremely helpful in my gathering facts for my book. I let her know that I have already photographed all 21 California Missions as well as the final resting place of Fr. Junipero Serra. We visited the church in Petra where Fr. Serra was an alter boy then headed back to Palma de Mallorca where the cab driver took us to the school where Fr, Serra was educated and the church of his first mass and the Cathedral in Palma with the large rose window.

On the way back to the ship we admired the waterfront of Palma with all it activity in elegant nightclubs and restaurants beckoning us to return to this beautiful island as often as possible.

This trip by ship has been wonderful and convinced us that allowing your disability to become justification for becoming a couch potato is an unnecessary cop-out. So far traveling with a wheelchair has been very satisfying. We learned that sometimes Debbie has enough energy in the morning to use the wheelchair as a walker and actually meet her friends without the need for anyone pushing her in the wheelchair. Using the wheelchair as a walker may only last a few minutes but it gives Debbie such a great feeling of independence which all her friends admire. Typically by mid-morning she is back in her wheelchair content to have me take her to lunch. I often find her a table by the pool where she can converse with friends.

Dinner is never a problem as the Dinning Room Staff is quite attentive to Debbie, they take the wheelchair from me to take her to her table, help her become seated, fold-up her wheelchair and return it to her when she is finished. They help her back into the wheelchair to escort her out of the dinning room to the elevators.

The real test will come when we dock at Civitavecchia (Rome) where we have a car rental waiting for us to visit cities where ships cannot go.

First Transatlantic Landfall, Azores

Auto, Train and Cruise Ship, comfortable with a wheelchair.

Cruise from Galveston, TX to Rome, Italy on Celebrity, MV Galaxy, 2006.

Auto trip From Rome, Italy to Florence, Reutte, Austria and on to Bavaria 2006.

Auto Trip from Munich, Germany to Salzberg and Vienna, Austria, 2006

Auto Trip after a week in Vienna to Bayreuth, Germany. 2006

Auto Trip from Bayreuth, Germany to Newschwanstein Castle in Bavaria, 2006

Auto Trip from Bavaria to Strasburg, Colmar and Beaunne, France, 2006

Auto trip from Beaunne in Wine Region to Chateau Region, France, 2006

Train trip from Blois France, to Paris France, 2006

Auto trip from Blois, France to Avignon, France, 2006

Auto trip from Avignon, France to Nice, France, 2006

Auto trip after 12 days in Nice to Monaco, Porto Fino and La Spezia, Italy, 2006

Auto trip to Orviato, Assisi and Rome Italy, 2006

Cruise from Athens, Greece to the Black Sea on Oceana, M/S Nautica, 2006

Cruise from Istanbul, Turkey to Venice, Italy on Oceana, M/S Nautica, 2006

Cruise from Venice, Italy to Barcelona, Spain on Oceana, M/S Nautica, 2006

Cruise from Copenhagen, Denmark to St. Petersburg, Russia, MS Amsterdam

Cruise from St. Petersburg Russia to Wanamunde, Germany, MS Amsterdam, 2006

Train trip from Wanamunde Germany to Berlin , Germany, 2006

Cruise from the Baltic Sea to New York City, HAL, MS Amsterdam, 2006

Cruise from Los Angeles, CA to Sydney Australia, Cunard, QE2, 2007

Cruise from Sydney, Australia to Dalian, China, HAL MS Statendam, 2007

Cruise from Hong Kong China to Athens, Greece, Oceana, Nautica, 2007

Auto trip from Piraeus to Delphi, Greece, 2007

Auto trip from Brussels, Belgium to Amsterdam, Netherlands, 2007

Auto trip from Amsterdam to Luxemburg, 2007

Auto trip from Luxemburg to Romantic Road and on to Munich , Germany, 2007

Auto trip from Liechtenstein and Switzerland to Lake Como, Italy, 2007

Auto trip from Como, Italy to Nice, France, for 9 more days, 2007

Cruise from Monaco to Harwich, England, HAL MS Rotterdam 6, 2007

Auto Trip from La Harve, France to Versaille and Paris, France, 2007

Auto trip from Cork, Ireland to Dingle , Ireland, 2007

Auto trip from Dingle, Ireland to Dublin, Ireland, 2007

Cruise from Southampton, England to New York, Cunard, HMS Queen Mary 2

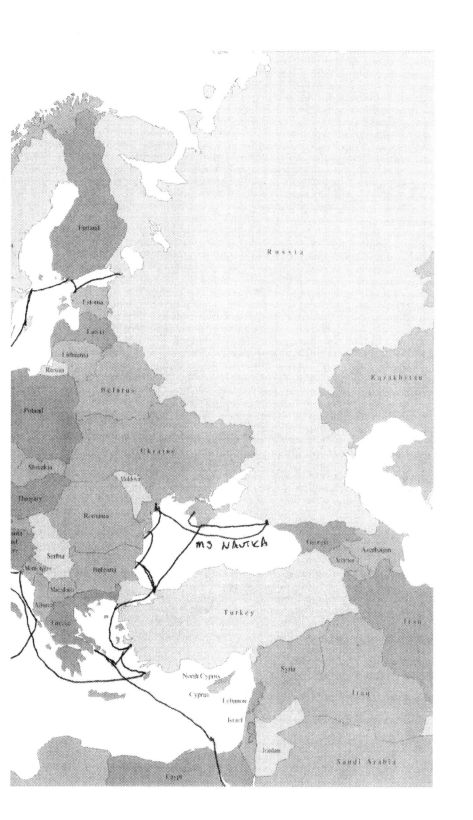

CHAPTER V

ITALY

Our plan was to have a home base in Italy with access to Rome and the various hill towns. We selected Oravieto, an Etruscan Hill Town about 60 miles north of Rome. The Celebrity ship Galaxy docked at Citavecchia and shortly thereafter we had Debbie's overabundance of luggage packed to the roof of a rental car, so much so that I could not use the rear view mirror. Soon we were passing beautiful lakes and heading for Oravieto.

Oravieto.

We checked into the Hotel Oravieto and met their wonderful staff. We let them know that we arrived by ship and wanted to use their hotel for a few days as our land headquarters both at the beginning of our six weeks on land and at the end as well. They were so hospitable they agreed to store our entire cruise luggage in their hotel for our six weeks travel on land.

With the car now empty of luggage, we thoroughly enjoyed the cafes, restaurants and history of Oravieto, the first of many Etruscan hill towns we visited. The food here is excellent, paper-thin pizza and an extraordinary array of Italian dishes found in so many restaurants in Oravieto.

A new adventure awaited us as we attempted to board a train in Oravieto for a day trip to Rome. The Oravieto Train Station had many tracks and platforms and our train was to arrive on a middle platform with many, many steps going down, then through a tunnel and up again to get to the next platform. The elevator was out or order and to our great surprise three strong rail employees picked up Debbie in her wheelchair and carried her across the tracks to the appropriate platform and set her down. Wow! What is lacking in technology is made up with heart. These people are wonderful.

Rome.

Upon arrival in Rome we took a cab to the Vatican and St Peter's Square, took in a mass, and stopped for a few beers in an outdoor café then proceeded to join the long line waiting to visit the Sistine Chapel. The line was about three hours long we were told as we finally got to the end of the line. Two nuns noticing Debbie in a wheelchair approached us and said we should go to the front of the line where you pay your entrance fee. We walked a few blocks to the front of the line and were immediately entered to the chapel and told there is no entrance fee for either of us. Another great example of Italian hospitality.

Michelangelo's paintings in the Sistine Chapel are awesome! "Creation" in the center of the ceiling exemplifies his talent.

With Debbie in her wheelchair we were able to see the Pantheon built in 27 BC, a marvel of architecture, the Roman Forum, the Coliseum which held 80,000 cheering spectators doing thumbs down each time the lions won, a lunch at the foot of the 137 Spanish Steps and throwing coins in the Fountain de Trevi to assure we would return to Rome again.

The afternoon was spent taking Debbie shopping. The owner of the fashion store where Debbie shopped recommended dinner at Caminetto, his favorite restaurant. We took his advice and had a gourmet dinner before boarding the train for our 45 minute ride trip back to Oravieto,

Upon arrival at Oravieto we noticed we were on the outside platform and the porters were already there waiting to help Debbie off the train. Oravieto is such a quiet place compared to Rome, and it seemed good to us to be back to such familiar surroundings.

After a cultural day in Rome and good night rest we were ready for another adventure.

Civita de Bagnoregio.

We checked out of the Hotel Oravieto, waved goodbye to the friendly staff and headed for a tiny Etruscan Hill town called Civita di Bagnoregio where we had made reservations in a B&B overlooking the town square. On the way we passed other hill towns but stayed on course until we saw before us a most imposing site.

"There it is Deb," I said.

Donkey Path, Civita di Bagnoregio, Italy

"My God! I'm not going up there", she said.

"There are no cars in Civita, I will have to push you up that goat path or donkey trail to the gate at the top. I see a place where we are supposed to park the car at the bottom."

"I think you should call and cancel the reservation," she offers.

"Let us at least try it," I suggested.

We park the car and unload the wheelchair and a single overnight bag that was placed on Debbie's lap and I commenced pushing the wheelchair up the donkey trail. We got part way and Debbie suggested I take a break as she heard me huffing and puffing. We stopped for a moment and put the breaks on the wheelchair.

"How are we ever going to get down from here", she asked.

"Let us get up to the top first, maybe they can lower us on a rope" I chuckled.

I started pushing again and we were about half way up we heard voices behind us, saying:

"Can we take it from here?"

I turned to look and found two young athletic men, an American and an Italian; both looked to me like body builders, compared to me at age 70.

I said, "welcome to the chariot race." They laughed and pushed the wheelchair near the top of the hill where another surprise was waiting for us.

The goat trail curves near the top, and was no longer a flat surface, and became pie shaped steps to go around the curve. Lots of pie shaped steps. The young men picked up Debbie in the wheelchair negotiated all the steps and placed the chair down under the gate marking the entrance to Civita di Bagnoregio.

"Hey guys, thank you, lets go the that café where I can buy you some beers."

"No thanks," they replied "We are happy to help". "Arrivaderci."

As we entered the town square we spotted another café, and ordered beers. Quaffing down a cold beer we noticed our B&B across the square, above the "Tratoria Antico Forno". The few rooms upstairs were being cleaned and a woman at an open window was leaning out banging her dust mop against the outside of the stone building. Each window had a flower box of red geraniums hang from the sill.

"I'll bet that is our room", Debbie said.

"Probably?" "We can't check in until noon so let's check out the rest of Civita." As we walked through this historic Etruscan Town we discovered the birthplace of St. Bonaventure, a small stone building, right on the edge of a cliff with great views of the farmlands far below the cliffs. In another tiny stone building an old man was making bruchetta over an open fire in his fireplace. He invited us to try some, which we did and found it delicious.

As we approached our B&B to check in we noticed stone steps at the entrance. As I parked the wheelchair behind a planter, Debbie was already sitting on the steps and with her arms lifting her buttocks up one step at a time. Where there is a will, there is a way, says it all about Debbie's endurance. Once through the door we checked in and now had to go up another set of stairs to the second floor. This staircase was a narrow staircase with a railing on both sides that Debbie using her arms again was able to ascend.

As we entered the room and looked out the window, Debbie laughed knowing she bet it would be the same room and window that we noticed the cleaning lady preparing for us.

From this window you could see the entire square, with the old Etruscan Church dominating the head of the square and its bell tower peeling off little bells every 15 minutes and the big bell on the hour every hour. The shops and café's across the square and the many orange tiled roofs atop the brown stone buildings bordering the rest of the town square.

In mid-afternoon, Debbie was taking a nap, I could hear a put-put sound and look out the window to see a vehicle which appears to be a motorcycle for the front wheel with two wheels in the back with a tiny truck body atop the two wheels.

"So that is how they get food and supplies up here" I thought.

We later went downstairs to "Tratoria Antico Forno" and Chef Franco Sala, came out to introduce himself.

"I know you", Debbie said.

"How is that possible", the chef responds.

'I see you on cooking shows in the United States."

"I didn't know I was on in the United States, I'll have to speak to my agent about that. It could be someone is showing one of my tapes in America.

The dinner that evening was excellent as expected, the friendly chef offered the services of the little cart I saw to take us down the goat trail the next day.

Toward noon the next day we heard the put-put of the little vehicle waiting to take us down to our car. The bumpy ride down the pie shaped steps is the reason for the single front wheel. Once we got to the flat surface it became easier but like a roller coaster ride nonetheless.

Thanking the driver as he dropped us off at our car we both looked up at this thirteenth century Etruscan town knowing that our experiences in Civita di Bagnoregio will last a lifetime.

Sienna

Heading North from Civita we stopped at Sienna a much larger hill town than Oravieto or Civita de Bagnorego. Sienna has many of the same characteristics of building a city on a hill that is easier to defend.

Sienna's Plaza Il Campo is definitely worth a visit. A giant square surrounded by restaurants and café's and impressive architecture.

Florence (Firenze)

This city of beautiful buildings with orange tiled roofs and so many bridges crossing the Arno River was during the 15th century the art and intellectual capital of Europe. Under the rule of the Medici family it was the leading city of the Renaissance world. There is so much art and architecture that you could easily spend a week visiting the many museums.

We arrived in Florence in late afternoon and walked along the river enjoying the architecture on both sides. There is just too much to see in Florence so on our next trip we plan to spend a few days.

Verona

Made famous by William Shakespeare's Romeo and Juliet we saw nothing as the weather turned bad and we decided to continue our journey to Reutte, Austria.

St. Peter's Basicila, Vatican City

Colosseum, Rome, Italy

Trevi Fountain, Rome

B&B on town Square in Civita di Bagnoregio, Italy

CHAPTER VI

AUSTRIA

Sometimes the best-laid plans do not work out. I have written both a screenplay and a book on Richard Wagner and his benefactor King Ludwig II of Bavaria, it was important to me to visit and see first hand the famous sites of both individuals to provide photo support for the book.

Ehrenberg.

In the Tyrol Region of Austria, we visited the ruins of the Ehrenberg Castle built 700 years ago during the time of the Crusades. Knights in armor defended the Tyrol Region of Austria from a castle high on the hilltop. We also visited the beautiful church in Ehrenberg before heading to Reutte, also in the Tyrol Region.

Reutte.

We arrived in Reutte, Austria, our home base for Bavaria in the late afternoon sunshine and checked into our hotel that provided us with a bedroom and separate study with a deck overlooking the Alps. The study was certainly a great place for a writer to become inspired.

The next morning the weather changed to rain. Reutte is only about 30 minutes from Neuschwanstein Castle in Germany, so we went anyway. I took photos in the rain of the castle that came out, as you would expect, dreary and not flattering.

Still raining the next day I went back to tour the inside of both castles and found them quite interesting and educational. That evening the rain turned to sleet which was our warning to leave Reutte as soon a possible as my friends will you, after leaving my home of 20 years in Vermont for La Jolla, California, John does not do snow! All kidding aside, Vermont is a wonderful place to bring up children and holds a special place in my heart, so much so that I wrote still another book titled, The Fourteenth State.

When the rain turns to sleet in Reutte we knew what to expect next so we came down from the mountains and headed for Munich and Lake Schoenberg, in Berg Germany where we stayed overnight as it continued to rain. It was obvious from the weather reports that we were in for an entire week of unrelenting rain. It is times like these that you have to adjust to the elements. This storm was heading across Europe from West to East. One of our longer rides planned was to visit Vienna, Austria. So as long as it is a long ride, why not do it now and once visited we head east again and travel the opposite direction of the storm and eventually punch through it into the sunshine,

Salzburg.

So with our plan revised, we headed for Salzburg made famous by Mozart. The car provided good shelter from the storm and we were quite safe on super highways as we made use of the storm to attain distance from Reutte listening to Mozart all the way.

Vienna.

Vienna, Austria is a beautiful city. Our hotel was central and we had no problems with the wheelchair. We were comfortable in Vienna, so we stayed seven days and watched the weather. With good restaurants, fantastic pastries, and the music of both Mozart and Johann Strauss, life is good.

A day in the middle of the week turned sunny due to holes in the clouds, so we took advantage of the sun and took a riverboat for a cruise on the Danube River. The blue Danube was brown because of all the rain in Europe. The river was also too high, closing roads between Vienna and Prague and Vienna and Budapest. The high river also prevented riverboats from sailing the Danube to these cities that we intended to visit by boat from Vienna.

We had our little sunshine on our Danube River Cruise; the captain even intentionally severely rocked the boat back and fourth to the Johan Strauss music, Blue Danube waltz and everyone on board laughed.

Mozart, Beethoven, Strauss, and Hayden all had homes in Vienna as well as did Sigmund Freud and may other artists and intellectuals as the city with all its gardens and palaces is often referred to as the Paris of Eastern Europe.

On our last day in Vienna we visited the Vienna Woods, which provided us with a hilltop view of the entire city. Before dinner we took photos of the Vienna Opera House, then had our Winerschnitzel and pastries and retired for the evening knowing tomorrow we would be departing for Germany.

CHAPTER VII

GERMANY

It was raining when we left Vienna but we knew we were traveling in the opposite direction as the storm. By the time we reached Nuremberg Germany we had already punched through the storm and had the complete long awaited sunshine.

Lunch in Nuremberg consisted of German sausage platter with lots of cold beer. It was World Cup time and the most advertised car on TV was the car we were in. Often when we returned to our car there were crowds around it peeking inside, this car appeared to be Fiat's answer to BMW and Mercedes Benz.

Bayreuth.

Our first objective in Germany was to visit Bayreuth, pronounced Bi Roit where Richard Wagner designed and had built his Festspielhaus for his Wagner Operas.

As we pulled into the parking lot of our Hotel in Bayreuth and unloaded the car I noticed a bubble in a tire of the car that could cause us a lot of trouble. After checking in the hotel the hotel manager helped by speaking German in a call to Auto Europe to have this tire replaced. Auto Europe sent a man out to pick up the car and get us a new tire.

Bayreuth is a very special beautiful well-groomed town. Richard Wagner's Festspeilhaus is the ultimate highlight set in a park that caused us both to be stunned in awe when we first approached it on this sunny day.

I was able to push the wheelchair from the hotel up the hill to the Festspeilhaus and then back down the hill to Wagner's home that contains many artifacts of Wagner's career.

Richard and Cosima Wagner are buried in the garden behind Haus Mansfried their home, quite unusual for Germany, but then again he is the town's most honored citizen.

When we returned to the hotel expecting to find our car we had a message that they do not have the proper tire and would give us a Volkswagen instead. We didn't bite; get us a tire was our reply.

The next day the hotel manager helped us again, by speaking in German, letting Auto Europe in Bayreuth know in no uncertain terms that only a tire was required and not an exchange of cars so that they can have the World Cup most advertised car at their disposal.

On the third day we had our new tire at a cost of $280.00 US dollars. One of the benefits of six weeks on land in Europe is you can retrace your steps that weather inhibited. We both agreed that Bavaria was worth a second chance, and headed right for Lake Starnberg and Berg Germany.

I wanted photos of Berg Castle where King Ludwig II spent his last days. Berg Castle is now owned privately and is walled off with high shrubs for privacy, so it cannot be seen. We stayed at the same B&B that we stayed last time, and this time we rented a boat and I went out on Lake Starnberg and took much better photos of both Berg Castle and the spot marking where King Ludwig drowned.

We retraced our steps to Neuschwanstein Castle in Bavaria and finally took decent photos of the beautiful romantic architecture of King Ludwig II. We stayed again overnight 30 minutes away in Reutte, Austria, but the next morning we were thrilled about taking photos in the sunshine, Linderhof Castle, and Obermanghou, and finally we head for Stuttgart.

We stayed in Stuttgart and watched the World Cup with the fans, because Germany was the sponsor in 2006. Needing to find a hotel for the night, I left Debbie in the car while inquiring at TI for a hotel. When I returned crowds continued to surround the car to ask how we like it.

A good sauerbraten meal and a fine night rest got us off to an early start the next morning to cross the Rhine heading for France.

Neuschawnstein Castle in bad weather

Neuschwanstein Castle

CHAPTER VIII

FRANCE

Beaunne.

Strasburg to Colmar to Beaunne is wine country in France, with so many nice cafes to visit. We stayed in a walled in hotel in Beaunne where they lock the gate at night so no one can get in or out. Each of these three towns provided us with new experiences and each of the three we would visit again.

Amboise.

In Amboise, France we saw our first Chateau. We met a wonderful couple with their teenagers from San Jose, CA who the next day made a date to meet us again at Chateau Chenenceau and Chateau Chamboise. Our home base for the Chateau Region was Blois, France.

Blois.

In 1973 I spent a week in Paris so I was quite familiar with the city and given we allocated only one day for Paris, I wanted Debbie to see some sights to remember. We left our home base Blois by train early in the morning and arrived in Paris, by 9:00 am

Paris.

Our first stop was the Muse D'Orsay where the French Impressionists art resides. Debbie and I were given the special treatment of no entrance fee and a wheelchair map showing all the elevators. Trust me, French hospitality exists. This might be a good place to point out that Frenchman is often given a bad rap. Just like in the few ugly Americans traveling in Europe with no manners, constantly demanding service give an impression that all Americans must be simular. In France you will find very warm and friendly people very proud of their country, wanting to help everyone, regardless of nationality.

Paris is wheelchair friendly; we were able to walk from Place de Concorde to the Arch de Triumph, to the Eiffel tower and along the parks along the Seine. For lunch it was a café along the Champs Elyessey where you could sit and people watch, as the Parisians so frequently do over a glass of wine. Debbie enjoyed writing her postcards from the relaxed environment of the cafes.

We returned to Blois by train for dinner and planned to leave the next morning by car for Nice, with an overnight stop in Avignon that is about half way to Nice from Blois.

Avignon.

The historic city of Avignon was at one time the residence of the Popes when the Papacy moved from Rome to Avignon. We stayed overnight in Avignon and understood its significance.

Nice.

Our plan was to spend two days in Nice and then fly to Ireland. We have never been to either place but when Debbie saw Nice, we decided to put Ireland off to next year and we stayed in Nice for twelve days. Nice is nice! Our hotel room and balcony overlooked the Mediterranean; the hotel staff was extremely helpful and pleasant.

When you stay twelve days pushing Debbie in a wheelchair along the Promenade des Angels, people get to know you and get used to seeing you. We had our favorite restaurants where the manager would greet us. We became familiar with a special hairdressing salon, and even the local Laundromat. Nice was so comfortable that we never used the car the entire time of our stay.

Even my nieces would think Nice is nice.

Eventually we had to leave and finally used the car again for our trip back to Italy.

Chateau Chennenceau, France

Train from Blois, to Paris, France

Apertif on the Champs Elisse, Paris, France

CHAPTER IX

SIX WEEKS ON LAND COMES TO A CONCLUSION

The objective of this trip is to return to Oravieto, Italy, pick up our Cruise luggage, drive to Rome, return the car rental and fly from Rome to Athens, Greece where we board the Oceania Cruise Ship M/S Nautica, for three back to back fifteen day cruises.

MONACO

While en-route to Italy we passed through Monaco and drove the famous Grand Prix de Monaco circuit before making our obligatory stop at the mother of all casinos, Casino de Monte Carlo.

The world famous Casino de Monte Carlo is distinctive in its feminine like architecture.

ITALY

Porto Fino, Italy.

As we enter the Italian Riverira, we plan to have lunch at Porto Fino, Italy. We know our Cruise Ship will be taking us there as well, but for now we stop in by car. The roads in and out of Porto Fino are very narrow and a driver must be very careful at every curve. Walking around Porto Fino was fun, a quaint little village with lots of restaurants on the sea. We had a great lunch and decided to continue to La Spezia, Italy a home base for the Cinque Terre Region.

La Spezia, Italy

Two of the five towns of the remote Cinque Terre were wheelchair accessible, but we never found the access road, got lost in the mountains, became tired and returned to our very comfortable hotel in La Spezia.

La Spezia is a beautiful town on the Mediterranean Sea. Some streets are blocked off and serve as malls with lots of restaurants and shopping. An evening in La Spezia was certainly a good time.

The next morning we decided not to try to access Cirque Terre Region by car but to take the train or boat on our next visit from La Spezia, we chose rather to head for Orvieto today and arrive earlier than expected.

We left La Spezia and arrived at the Oravieto hotel before noon. We stayed three nights before heading to the airport with our luggage.

Assisi, Italy

One of the days in Oravieto we took a side trip to Assisi, another Hill Town in Umbria and home of St. Francis, the patron saint of Italy,

Finally we arrive at Leonardo de Vinci Airport in Rome with our luggage checked in for Athens. Cruise Ship luggage again became a problem as Olympic Airways charged us for excess baggage.

The short flight to Athens fit our criterion of keeping flights as short as possible.

Casino de Monte Carlo, Monaco

CHAPTER X

THE BLACK SEA

OCEANA, M/S NAUTICA

This is the first of three Cruises on the Oceania Cruise Lines, M/S Nautica. When you book back to back cruises you normally pick up an extra day in the port where passengers are disembarking. We love the idea of having this Black Sea Cruise ending in Istanbul, giving us three days to explore this great city that is half in Asia and half in Europe. The morning of the middle day is when travelers disembark and the next afternoon is when new travelers get on board.

Santorini, Greece.

Our first port of call was the Greek Island of Santorini. NOT WHEELCHAIR FRIENDLY. The island is picturesque because the whitewashed homes are built on the rim of a volcano, which the ocean had filled. The ship enters the volcano through one of the openings to the sea.

The ship brings you ashore by tender and when Debbie who can not step off a curb without a panic of trembling and holding my arm so tightly saw the step from the ship to the tender going up and down while rocking in the waves, she declined to go and wanted me to go and take photos.

She had many offers to lift her on board the tender, which she declined, because it will remain with her as far worse than stepping off a curb.

Santorini involves, getting ashore, traveling up a funicular to the rim and walking up and down many steps following each contour of the volcano's rim admiring all the whitewashed buildings with blue trim.

Santorini, is the first instance on this trip of something Debbie in her condition cannot do, and it appears two-fold, boarding a ships tender. We put men on the moon and still have not designed a way to put a wheelchair person on a tender. Fortunately, most of the ports we visit will have docks, but now we know disabled persons should be aware that although ships are the preferred way to travel, inquire before you book how many port have docks. It turns out that even if Debbie did get ashore, Santorini is definitely not a wheelchair friendly place and there are steps everywhere following the curvature of the volcano.

TURKEY

Kushadasi Turkey was our next port with a dock waiting for our ship. We had read about the ancient city of Ephasus and new beforehand that it would not be wheel chair friendly. Debbie insisted that I go and take photos while she got her hair done aboard ship.

Ephesus.

I hired a cab and toured the ancient city on foot. Ephesus is the city where St. Paul preached to the Ephesians. The front wall of the Library of Ephesus is still standing and many homes of the residents are still in reasonable condition.

On the way back to the ship I took photos of ruins of the Temple of Artimus one of the Seven Ancient Wonders of the World and photos of the last home of the Virgin Mary, that Pope John Paul II after his visit, declared it authentic and worthy of a pilgrimage.

Debbie enjoyed the photos of these three famous sites back on board the ship as we entered the Dardennels on our way to the Black Sea.

UKRAINE

Yalta

Our first Black Sea Port is Yalta in the Ukraine made famous by the famous World War II Yalta Conference where Roosevelt, Churchill and Stalin agreed to divide up and reconstruct Europe after the war.

Yalta is a beautiful city; our cab driver toured the city for us and dropped us of at the palace where we saw all the photos and memorabilia of the famous conference.

Sevastopol

Sevastopol, in the Ukraine is quite beautiful. Access was again easy we were able to walk everywhere with the wheelchair. There are many war monuments in Sevastopol and we took many photos of children with their parents on a Sunday afternoon in this festive city.

Odessa.

Odessa was our favorite city in the Ukraine. Even the Cruise Ship Terminal is impressive with a major hotel and chapel at the end of the pier. We had lunch at the Mozart Café across the street from the Odessa Opera House. A violinist on the street was playing Mozart's concerti as the local residents walked by. We spent the entire day walking the streets of Odessa, talking with the residents and visiting the shops and occasionally enjoying a beer or a glass of wine. The young women of Odessa dress just like young women in San Diego, CA, very modern, upbeat clothing.

RUSSIA

Sochi, Russia

The day after visiting Yalta we visited Sochi, Russia that also had dock making access easy. At the time of our visit Sochi was being considered as a site for the Olympic Games.

ROMANIA

Constanta, Romania is still has some streets in disrepair. The cobblestone streets have potholes in town that we were able to negotiate, however once you get to the waterfront on the Black Sea, everything is well groomed. The promenade along the sea is quite beautiful and well worth a walk. The beautiful circular casino still serves elegant dinners in the ballroom. We found an outdoor café with umbrellas along the promenade and decided to spend the afternoon there watching the surf pound the rocks and the swimmers sunning themselves on the beach.

BULGARIA

Nesebur, Bulgaria, has its Old Town, which has been declared by UNESCO a World Heritage Site. The buildings of Old Town typically have stone first and wooden second floors, making them quite unique. We walked through all of Old Town admiring the unique architecture and found a café to talk with the residents to learn about their interesting culture before leaving Nesebur.

TURKEY

Istanbul.

As the ship leaves the Black Sea it enters the Bosphorus on its way to Istanbul, The Bosphorus is like a river with homes of the wealthy on both sides Many people are on deck to witness the beauty of the mansions along the way.

As we approach Istanbul large suspension bridges are before us connecting the Asian side of Istanbul with the European side. As we pass under the bridges you can see the minarets of the many mosques on shore.

Our Black Sea Cruise ends in Istanbul, Turkey. Because we continue on with back-to-back cruises we benefit with three full days in Istanbul.

The first day we took a cab to the Blue Mosque and the Hippodrome where years ago people cheered for the chariot racing. The second day we visited Suleyman Mosque and the famous Turkish Bazaar. The bazaar was so huge we never did see it all, but certainly got to talk to a lot of Turks and found them to be so cordial. One person outside the Bazaar saw Debbie in her wheelchair, told her she is beautiful, and gave her a free bracelet to guard her the rest of our trip.

The third day was our last day in Istanbul as new people started boarding the ship in the afternoon bound for a 15 day cruise from Istanbul to Venice.

Site of Yalta Conference, Yalta, Ukraine

Enjoying the Black Sea, Constanta, Romania.

Opera House, Odessa, Ukraine

Aboard ship, Oceana Nautica

CHAPTER XI

ISTANBUL TO VENICE
OCEANA, M/S NAUTICA

As we leave Istanbul and enter the Sea of Marma I am in the library of the ship trying to determine the exact location of the city of Troy.   I knew it would be on the south side of the Dardenelles and I wanted to make sure I saw Troy as we passed.

We left the wide Sea of Marma and entered the narrow Dardenels, and I figured Troy must be at the narrowest spot, so we waited and sure enough, marked by a Turkish Flag at the top of the hill was Troy, a city so many thought never existed and was just a fable of Homer's Iliad until Henry and Sophia Schliemann found the city.

Our first port is Kushadasi that we previously visited on this ship. This time however, I wanted Debbie to get ashore as Kushadasi is a wheel chair accessible city. We hired the same cab driver that took me to the east to Ephasus. This time we asked him to take us South so we could explore more of Turkey.

We headed for the historic site of Prene, a town that lay in ruins atop a large hill for defense, much like the hill towns of Italy, except that Alexander the Great designed this town and actually lived here awhile.

The terrain was too rough for a wheelchair, so Debbie waited in the cab while I climbed the hill and took photos to show her.

The cab driver offered to take us to a nearby National Park, but we chose to return to Kushadasi, which I knew was wheelchair accessible. We had lunch in the Kushadasi Bazaar called a Shush kabob for a Sultan. It was excellent. Debbie shopped all afternoon at the Bazaar and enjoyed the city of Kushadasi,

Rhodes, Greece.

Rhodes, Greece the next port of call is an island walled city from the time of the Crusades and full of history. The site of the Colossus of Rhodes one of the Ancient Seven Ancient Wonders of the World is on this island. Some believe the Colossus actually straddled the harbor entrance with ships passing between his legs. There is currently a promotion to raise funds to re-build the Colossus of Rhodes.

Mykonos, Greece.

Mykonos, Greece with its whitewashed buildings with their ubiquitous blue trim and windmills moving in the breeze, and so many narrow alleys creating a labyrinth of adventure is my favorite Greek Island. I stayed a few days here in 1975 and wanted to make sure Debbie sees how beautiful it is. We shopped in the alleys and stopped at a Greek Taverna with mandolins playing and enjoyed the unusually heavy surf as this day was a windy one. After lunch in still another taverna where Debbie was writing postcards, the ships horn sounded three times, and staffs from the ship were in town gathering people to return because the captain of the ship wanted to depart before the high winds picked up additional speed.

Santorini, Greece.

Santorini, Greece. Once again we visit this Island. This time, rather than go ashore I stayed on board the ship with Debbie and took in some ship activities.

Athens, Greece.

Athens, Greece. The nice couple from San Jose, CA when we had dinner at Chateau Amboise in France asked me if I had been to Athens and I said I spent a week there. They asked me if I did the Archeological Museum and I said no. They convinced me that it is a must see Museum. At the dock we met Cosmos, a cab driver that we hired for the entire day. I have visited Athens before and knew the sights to show Debbie and Cosmos took us to all of them, we invited Cosmos to lunch at a taverna in the Plaka and he explained the significance of this very old section of Athens

The highlights of Athens are of course the Parthenon and the Acropolis where we took photos and we later visited the National Archeological Museum as instructed. Museum guides directed us to a separate wheelchair entrance, as we approached the ticket booth they said there is no charge for those with wheelchairs.

Once inside the National Archeological Museum, we found the couple from San Jose, CA to be correct. This museum is another must see. Artifacts from the discovered city of Troy are there for anyone to see. The death mask of Agamemnon made of gold is also on display around many fascinating Greek pieces of antiquity.

Cosmos was waiting with his cab for us so we only spent one hour exploring the treasures of this museum. As soon as we left Cosmos was there to take is back to the ship in Piraeus. We both love Greek food so we asked Cosmos to drop us off where all the waterfront restaurants are in Piraeus so we could have dinner. There must be twenty restaurants in a row facing the harbor in Piraeus. We walked by each of them and noticed they all had three to five steps down from the sidewalk to enter the restaurant and one of them had a ramp. So where do you think we had dinner, the quaint little Greek restaurant with that ramp that the wheelchair could access.

We sailed out of Piraeus bound for the mountainous Amalfi coast of Italy. Then back to Naxos, Sicily, with Mt. Etna smoking as I went ashore by tender.

MONTENAGRO.

Kotor, Montenegro was our next port, located at the end of the Southern most fjords in Europe. Some of the ships officers wanted to by property in Kotor and we understood. Kotor is a beautiful quiet place with mountains all around, good for boating and a World Heritage Site as well.

CROATIA.

Dubrovnik, Croatia our next port on the Adriatic Sea is a walled City with a lot of charm.

Stone buildings, a beautiful church, many alleys, and fine restaurants and of course still another World Heritage Site.

Leaving Dubrovnic we head North in the Adriatic Sea anticipating sighting our next port that starts as a speck on the horizon that grows larger as we finally make out the tower of St. Marks Square.

ITALY

Venice

What a wonderful way to enter Venice, Italy as you pass the buoys, the levy under construction to control water levels and finally the fort protecting the harbor. Once past the fort the view of Venice is spectacular, in a wide canal for big ships you pass the Basilica, the Grand Canal, St. Marks Square and head for the docks at the Northern part of the city. Most passengers disembark on the second day while new passengers embark in the afternoon of the third day. We have three days to explore Venice as we stay on the ship for our second back-to-back cruise on the Oceana Nautica.

Three days in Venice was perfect with cafes, restaurants, the Opera House, the many shops, the costumes and masks everywhere. The highlight for me was an invitation to the Richard Wagner apartment on the Grand Canal where I could gather data for my book, *Truimph of the Swan,* a Biographical Novel of Composer Richard Wagner and King Ludwig II of Bavaria.

The Blue Mosque, Istanbul, Turkey

Suleymaniye Mosque, Istanbul, Turkey

Inside the Grand Bazaar, Istanbul, Turkey

Friendly Turk gave Debbie a bracelet, Istanbul, Turkey

Sultan's Sush-ke-bob, Kusadasi, Turkey

Library at Ephasus, Turkey

Alexander the Great, lived for a time here in Prene, Turkey

Mykonos, Greece

Oceana Nautica passing St.Marks Square, Venice, Italy

CHAPTER XII

VENICE TO BARCELONA
OCEANA, M/S NAUTICA

It was not easy to leave Venice, such a unique city, previously visited by so many famous literary people, composers, artists etc. I can see why. Venice is an intellectual must!

On our six weeks on land we did the interior of Italy including many hill towns, this cruise will take us to many of the seaside ports of Italy. We started in Venice and will head around the foot of Italy to such ports as Sorrento, Amalfi, Rome (Civitaveccia) Liverno, Porto Fino, thus combined with our trips on land by car; we have deep feelings for Italy.

Sailing South on the Adriatic Sea, our first port of call is Dubrovnic, Croatia again, followed by the Greek Island of Corfu in the Ionian Sea and around the foot of Italy for a two-day visit in Sorrento, Italy.

Debbie had many friends on the ship and was content to stay aboard in Sorrento. I shared a cab with a wonderful couple from Arkansas to visit Pompeii, Italy the city that was destroyed by the Volcano Mt. Vesuvius. Pompeii was educational, interesting and very hot. The curbs were sometimes a foot high with chariot ruts in the stone streets. No place for Debbie at all, she stayed comfortable on the ship while I took photos to bring back to her.

Capri, Italy. The Isle of Capri required taking a boat from Sorrento that I did on the second day. Nice Restaurants a pretty beach and a funicular to the top of the mountain and fancy shops were the highlights.

Our ship leaves Sorrento for a return to Amalfi and Rome, (Civitavecci) and the French Island of Corsica.

Corsica.

Corsica, the Birthplace of Napoleon Bonaparte, is intriguing. I visited his childhood home. Corsica is very beautiful and a fun place to visit. There are many, many outdoor cafes and restaurants. Residents sit and people watch as hundreds go by, shopping, going to work or heading for the beach. We are curious that Napoleon never went back to this wonderful place.

Porto Fino, Italy. As we enter the tiny harbor of Porto Fino we see the tenders getting ready to take passengers ashore. We were so thankful that we did Porto Fino by car previously because Debbie cannot board a tender. We both stayed on the ship that day knowing we already had a good time in Porto Fino.

Monte Carlo, Monaco.

The ship docked within walking distance of the cafes and shopping so we had lunch by the sea and continued on to the famous Monte Carlo Casino. Sure we gambled and lost but marveled at the opulence of this mother of all casinos, with chandeliers, and first class service available to all that entered.

Marseille, France

We expected a busy seaport city and had no idea how much we were to enjoy Marseille. We walked many miles through closed streets turned into malls, back and fourth comparing prices and finally sat and relaxed at a waterfront restaurant. Debbie started writing post cards while enjoying some French wine and watch the passers by.

Barcelona, Spain.

Earlier on this cruise we inquired about a 35-day cruise on Oceana, Nautica for 2007 from Hong, Kong to Athens with the question, how many ports have docks rather than tenders. Before we disembarked we received the answer, all the ports have docks and no port will require a tender.

We disembarked the Oceana, Nautica in Barcelona, and took a cab to the airport for a flight to Copenhagen, Denmark.

CHAPTER XIII

THE BALTIC SEA, COPENHAGEN TO ST. PETERSBURG HOLLAND AMERICA, MS AMSTERDAM

Our timely and uneventful flight arrived in Copenhagen on schedule. Our cab driver gave us a tour of Copenhagen prior to our boarding Holland America's flagship, MS Amsterdam.

Our first port of call Tallinn, Estonia during a rainstorm, so we stayed on board the ship observing the city from the distance.

RUSSIA.

St. Petersburg, Russia

Without a prearranged visa which we did not have time to obtain, a person can enter Russia only if they are part of a tour group. As much as we dislike organized tours I had no alternative if I wanted to get photos of the Mariinski Theatre for my book to be titled *The Mighty Kuchka,* about Nikolai Rinsky-Korsakov and the Russian Five. So I signed up for three different tours.

The first tour was a St. Petersburg City Tour that drove by the Mariinski Theatre without stopping necessitating taking a photo of the Mariinski Theatre through a bus window that came out as you would expect, poor!

Before boarding the second tour bus I asked the tour guide if the bus could stop at the Mariinski Theatre for a few photos. She said maybe on the way back. On the return the bus went right by the theatre and didn't stop.

The third tour was an evening tour to an opera concert held at Yosopov Palace and again the bus passed the Mariinski Theatre on the way and I counted the number of blocks and turns until we got to Yosopov Palace. As the concert goers got off the bus, I asked the tour guide if I could walk the three enormous blocks to the Mariinski Theatre to take photos, she said maybe after the concert.

The concert was performed by the St. Petersburg Opera Company and many beautiful arias were performed. The concert was followed by a tour through Yosopov Palace where Rasputin was murdered. The precise room where Rasputin was poisoned contained wax figures of the characters involved in the crime plot, which was quite interesting. Before leaving Yosopov Palace there was an opportunity to shop for souvenirs of St. Petersburg that is such a beautiful city with so much to offer the visitor.

"Now is my chance" I thought.

I asked a fellow San Diegan to delay her souvenir shopping to hold up the bus while I go three blocks to take pictures of the Mariinski Theatre,

"I'll try", she said. "People will get angry if I hold the bus up too long."

I left the Palace and headed for the Mariinski theatre at 10:30 at night, but there is some daylight as St. Petersburg is so far north.

As I approached the theatre hundreds of people were coming out. They are quite well dressed. The Kirov ballet has just finished a performance. I decided to enter the theater by walking in backwards as people are coming out. Once in the theater I took photos for my book. I left the theatre and crossed the street and took pictures of a statue of Glinka, the father of Russian Music and started to return to the Palace to board the bus when a block later I passed a park to behold a magnificent statue of Nikolai Rimsky-Korsakov who is the lead character of my biographical novel.

Now with a camera containing many photos valuable to me I crossed another street and heard a loud horn attracting my attention. It was the tour bus that had parked, the driver was waving at me and opened its door to let me board. I got many dirty looks as I boarded the bus and the bus crossed the street to pick up the tour guide who was looking for me in front of the Mariinski Theatre. Irate passengers on the bus said I was lucky I did not end up in Siberia, walking around is a suit and tie with a camera with no passport.

As we approached our ship and got off the bus I apologized to the tour guide, gave her a big tip and thanked her for remembering that I wanted photos of the Mariinski Theatre.

FINLAND.

Helsinki, Finland

It was a bright sunny day when we docked in Helsinki. The city is so beautiful and the people so very friendly as most speak English and welcome Americans. Helsinki is noted for its revival in architecture and there are many fine examples. It was time to empty my camera to take new photos and put the St. Petersburg photos safely on disc. Our first stop was a photo shop in a mall that transferred the photos to disc while Debbie waited outside. A few minutes later after reviewing the photos on the disc I returned with the disc and gave it to Debbie to put in her bag. Our next stop was lunch at one of the many outdoor café's on the streets of Helsinki. While waiting for our lunch I erased all the St. Petersburg photos so I could now use the camera for Helsinki photos.

We visited the new Helsinki Opera House, took a tour and had lunch on the terrace overlooking the lake and park that also contains Finlandia Symphony Hall both are architectural achievements that I photographed and planned to walk to the Statue of the Finn composer Sibilius but Debbie was tiring so we will get that one next time.

At the Opera House I asked for a cold Finn beer, and the bar maid said, how's Lapin Kulta from Lapland in the far north where the reindeer live. I guess that will be cold enough, I'll take two, one with a glass.

Helsinki is wheelchair friendly on one side of the main street which shows they are aware of the need. The new Opera House, and symphony hall are both worth a visit.

SWEDEN.

Stockholm, Sweden.

We arrived in Stockholm the next morning, and I asked Debbie for the CD she has in her carryon bag. She emptied her bag and it was not there. We looked all over our cabin to no avail. The 227 photos most of St. Petersburg that some travelers say that I could have been banished to Siberia for walking the streets without a passport are lost.

I spent the entire morning trying to recover from this disaster. With a little luck I found a tiny cash register receipt from the photo store in Helsinki. After many attempts I got through to Anne, the young lady who waited on me for the CD. She said "I'm glad you called because someone found your CD on the ground next to where a woman was sitting in a wheelchair." If you give me your home address I will have the CD waiting for you by the time you return. Sure enough, when I got home the CD was there. Talk about snatching victory from the very jaws of defeat, thanks to Anne and Finn hospitality.

If you do not try to recover from disaster, you will certainly fail. With the 227 photos recovered, we can now enjoy our visit in Stockholm.

A sunny day in this city of the Nobel Prize, it must be a coincidence that the bus from the ship left me off in front of the Opera House. From the Mariinski Theatre, to Helsinki Opera House to the Stockholm Opera House, there must be a hidden message if I can figure it out. After visiting the outdoor cafes and Stockholm's Old town I just might have found the answer, it has to do with a book I sent to my publisher titled, "Triumph of the Swan". A Biographical Novel of Richard Wagner and King Ludwig II.

As I crossed a bridge on the way back to the Opera House I noticed in the lake below so many swans, some so elegant and others with their head straight down in the water with their rear end sticking up while finding food, looking not so elegant at all.

I tried to get a good photo of a graceful swan close up, but every time just before the click of my camera, the head would go quickly down deep in the water and my photos are buttocks and feet.

So is it a coincidence that I am standing in front of the Opera House near so many swans waiting for the bus that will take me back to the ship?

Visby, Sweden.

Visby is located on the West Coast of Gotland Island, Sweden's largest island.

UNESCO declared Visby a World Heritage Site to preserve the 13th century medieval architecture and relics from the Bronze age. Visby is a walled city to protect itself from invaders. A beautiful place to visit in an elegant park like setting.

GERMANY

Wanamunde, Germany.

Wanamunde is a resort on the North Sea near Rostock, Germany. It is a seaport where travelers can disembark to visit Berlin, which they typically do by tour bus. In the spirit of adventure, I took the train from Wanamunde to Berlin round trip for 32 Euros. The four-hour train ride with no English spoken allowed me to see the countryside of what was previously East Germany behind the Iron Curtain from 1945 to 1990. The area remains depressed in 2006 with graffiti on closed railway stations.

Berlin, Germany

About one half hour north of Berlin the view from the train showed a lot more prosperity. The buildings and parks are all well maintained and finally the train entered a most beautiful train station, The Berlin Train Station was built to coincide with the 2006 World Cup held in Germany. This train station is a marvel in architecture and is probably the most modern train station in the world. The exterior of glass lets the outside in, while the station interior has many levels of shops and boutiques, and even a supermarket as well as high end fashion stores and restaurants. Certainly the Berlin Train Station serves an example to others of what a train station can be in the future.

Immediately outside the Train Station is the Reichstag on the Platz de Republic that was repaired after a questionable fire in 1933 and suffered severe damage by the Red Army in 1945. With the fall of the Berlin Wall the Reichstag once again became the home of Germany's Parliament.

Just beyond the Reichstag is the Brandenburg Gate, the only remaining gate out of thirteen that were destroyed by Napoleon. The gate completed in 1791 supported with Greek Doric Columns the statue of the Goddess Victoria and her four stallions driving her chariot home after her triumph. This sculpture is absolutely beautiful and the Brandenburg Gate has become the national Symbol of Germany signifying its re-unification after the Cold War.

The Brandenburg Gate faces Unter den Linden (1000 Linden Trees) Avenue, a main thoroughfare in Berlin that runs from the Brandenburg Gate to the Palace. Walking this beautiful street is exhilarating with lunch at the Einstein Café and people watching makes you think of the musical "Cabaret". Berliners speak English as well as German and other languages and welcome Americans to the capital and cultural center of Germany.

No visit to Berlin would be complete without time spent on Museum Island, a UNESCO World Heritage Site. The Pergamon Museum contains the Pergamom Alter created in 170 BC in Asia Minor in honor of Zeus and Athena and more importantly is a relic of one of the Ancient Seven Wonders of the Ancient World.

The bust of Queen Nefetiti dates from 1350 BC that I saw in the Staatliche Museum, which contains Germany's great collection of Egyptology Relics and ranks as one of the best Egyptology Museums in the world. I am so glad I came to this museum because it only reinforces my desire to someday visit Egypt to see more of their history.

Berlin is a city of culture with the Duetche Opera Berlin attracting more than 300,000 theatre goers a year and is only one of many opera houses in Berlin.

The world class Berlin Philharmonic Orchestra established in 1887 with its history of famous conductors such as von Bulow, Nikisch, Furtwangler, von Karajan, Abado and Sir Simon Rattle stirs up memories of great concerts.

Berlin should not be missed on any visit to Germany.

This day ended with a train ride back to Warnemunde where people were enjoying their time in this resort town on the Baltic Sea with Holland America Ship Amsterdam preparing to depart giving us so many fond memories of Berlin.

DENMARK

Aarhus, Denmark

Aarhaus, is Denmark's second largest city and was established in 940 AD as a Viking settlement. Today the city has a population of 250,000 with lots of red brick buildings dominated by a huge Gothic church in the center of town. Some streets are cobblestone and others are closed off for pedestrian shopping.

Copenhagen, Denmark

Tivoli Gardens is a main attraction as is the Nyhaun Canal that is lined with bars and nightlife. The statues of "The Little Mermaid" in honor of Hans Christian Anderson the Danish author of so many fairy tales and called Copenhagen his home.

We did drink our share of Tuborg Beer, brewed in Denmark while visiting Copenhagen.

Still on the same ship we embark from Copenhagen for New York in a voyage across the North Atlantic. Keeping in mind that we only fly when absolutely necessary, we were fortunate to be booked on this ship because Heathrow airport was closed for a few days due to terrorist activity causing major backup of tourists sleeping in London's largest airport.

Mariinski Theatre, St. Petersburg, Russia

Cathedral of the Resurection, St. Pertersburg, Russia

CHAPTER XIV

TRANS-ATLANTIC COPENHAGEN TO NEW YORK HOLLAND AMERICA, MS AMSTERDAM

NORWAY.

Oslo, Norway.

With more than 1000 years of history Oslo is the oldest of the Nordic Capitols. The city is surrounded by islands and forests and is located on one of Norway's beautiful fjords. The shopping malls and waterfront restaurants are of every variety.

My extensive background in sailing and interests in explorers led me to the Viking Ship Museum that contains the best-preserved Viking Ships ever found. The ships were preserved in a bog and discovered in three royal burial grounds by the Oslo Fjord. My trip to this museum and actually touching these Viking Ships made me realize the Vikings ability to reach America as early as the year 850 or 900 with a speed of about 12 knots. Awesome to say the least and powerful evidence to start our transatlantic voyage from Norway to Iceland to Greenland and on to America, we are both excited.

The Oseberg Viking Ship has 15 oar holes on each side indicating 30 oarsmen, a helmsman and possibly a lookout and captain for a minimum total of 33 crew and captain. It is assumed that the crew slept in tents and did their cooking on land as well as suggested by the two cauldrons found on board hanging from collapsible tripods.

More contemporary is Norway's Thor Heyerdahl who in 1947 launched the Kon Tiki expedition. I was eleven years old and attending Richard E. Byrd school named after the great explorer of Antarctica and the South Pole when Thor Heyerdahl started his Kon Tiki adventure that really captured my interest. Thor Heyerdahl crossed from Peru to Polynesia on a balsa wood raft making 5000 miles in 101 days, proving that Polynesia was indeed within range of balsa wood rafts common to South America.

Years later I read the book, Kon Tiki and now I stand before the original balsa wood raft in the Kon Tiki Museum. Also on display are his Egyptian reed rafts RA1 and RA2 built at the foot of the Pyramids and dragged to Morocco where a successful sail from Africa to Barbados was completed in 57 days. Ra1 had flaws and was replaced by RA2 that completed the 4000-mile voyage.

Both the Viking Ship and Kon Tiki Museums are spectacular and contain artifacts, history and examples of Norwegian exploration.

Kristiansand, Norway

At the southernmost tip of Norway Kristiansand is the closest city to Denmark. It is a very clean city with upscale shopping and open malls closed to vehicular traffic. The Kristiansand Cathedral built in 1885 is neogothic in style and is Norway's largest church.

The city is well manicured in every detail and a very pleasant place to visit.

Bergen, Norway

The entrance to Bergen Harbor is preceded by the 30-mile Hjelterfjord and quite a beautiful cruise. The ship often travels under high suspension bridges between cliffs 2000 feet high and in some places there are wooden homes at the foot of the cliffs on the shore.

Bergen was the largest and most important town in Medieval Norway and today it ranks as Norway's second largest city. The Hanseatic League controlled trading for 200 years and built many sharply gabled houses around the harbor and many warehouses which have been declared a UNESCO World Heritage Site.

FAEROE ISLANDS

The Faeroe Islands are a territory of Denmark located in the North Atlantic Ocean between the Shetland Islands and Iceland.

Storytellers traveled throughout England repeating tales of King Arthur while in Ireland the professional storytellers told the adventure story of St. Brendan.

St. Patrick left Wales bound for Ireland to convert the Irish to Christianity. St. Brendan was one of St. Patrick's converts and was intelligent and well traveled. The Faeroe Islands play an important part of the story of St. Brendan that he recorded in Latin by hand in his book Navigato.

At age 70, St Brendan set sail for the promised land. By his own account in his own handwriting of which 120 copies still exist he describes the voyage to the promised land in such detail like witnessing fire and molton rocks rising from the sea. Volcanoes off the coast of Iceland are continually forming new islands.

St. Brendan's voyage took 7 years and it is believed he sailed from Ireland to the Faeroe Islands then on to Iceland and Newfoundland, Canada. Hard evidence is lacking, so it is difficult to conclusively prove Brendan's story, however scientists have not given up and the future discoveries may prove otherwise. If the story is true, that would put St. Brendan's discovery of America on or about the year 530.

Eighteen islands make up the Faeroe Islands which contain evidence of monks raising sheep at the time of St. Brendan. Before the Vikings from Scandinavia there were Norsemen who left the regimentation of civilization and set out to find new lands. There still remains plenty of sheep in the Faeroe Islands.

In 1976 after diligent research by Tim Severin who realized that the prevailing winds could possibly move a primitive boat from Ireland to the Faeroe Islands, then on to Iceland and Newfoundland, Canada. Tim set out to test his theory.

In County Kerry, Ireland Tim Severin found Irishmen using a medieval boat which he recreated using ox skin over an oak skeleton. Lines and sails were made from flax keeping with products of medieval times.

In 1776, Tim Severin and four companions set sail from Ireland to the Faeroe islands and as expected the prevailing winds made their voyage without incident in a timely manner. Brendan's Navigato refers to these islands as sheep islands. The first part of the Navigato seems to be correct.

From the Faeroe Islands it took twelve days to sail to Iceland where they witnessed newly formed volcanoes off the coast. So far Brandan's Navigato seems to hold true to the test.

Once in Iceland, Tim took the winter off waiting for the prevailing currents that took him to Newfoundland, Canada.

Thus Tim Severin was able to prove the possibility that Brendon's voyage reported in his Navigato was certainly possible. Other than the exaggeration of dinning on a whale's back added for the Irish Story Tellers the Navigato seems credible.

Remembering that these stories were written based on truth for professional storytellers that traveled throughout Ireland keeping the population entertained. Tim was sure he saw a whale large enough to dine on its back as well as for volcanoes spewing fire and smoke off the coast of Iceland; no Irishmen had ever seen fire coming out of the sea. The Navitago also discusses fog, dense fog that Newfoundland is noted for.

Like Thor Heyerdahl, who proved the possibility of a voyage on a balsa raft from Peru to Polynesia, Tim Severin has proved the possibility that St. Brendan could have arrived in a medieval ox skin sailboat from Ireland to Newfoundland, Canada.

We visited Torshavn a port city in the Faeroe Islands that exports fish and wool. The Faeore Islands are also spelled Faroe Islands and there are plenty of sheep as reported in the Navigato.

ICELAND

Akureyre, Iceland

The Vikings arrived here in 890 and by 1562 Akureyre became recognized as the second largest town in Iceland. Akureyri is on the north side of Iceland which was quite baron.

Trees were planted in 1952 and today Akureyri is very green at the foot of a 52-mile fjord with 3000-foot mountains.

Norsemen would have their land confiscated for various crimes so criminals looking for new land to replace what was lost settled Iceland. The Norsemen were farmers and brought sheep with them and they proceeded to learn fishing as well. These new settlers established themselves along the coastline of Iceland, as the interior is volcanic and not suitable for farming.

Prior to entering the beautiful fjord the ship Amsterdam crossed the Arctic Circle, so I have accomplished this feat twice, the first time in 1959 when I traveled to Point Barrow, Alaska. Each time it is a thrill.

"Helgi the lean" was first to sail up the 50-mile fjord in the 9th century where he established his farm. Akureri means "cornfield on the beach" at the head of the fjord and today it is quite beautiful. Walking through the town of Akureuri we found it immaculate and quite inviting with very friendly people.

Isafjordur, Iceland.

The west fjords are linked to the mainland by an isthmus and are the least visited parts of Iceland. Isafjordur has been a trading center since 1569 and is one of Iceland's largest fishing centers with 2900 residents. As we approach by ship from the sea we notice the towering peaks that shelter the harbor. Isafjordur is nestled at the foot of these peaks on Iceland's north shore.

Reykjavik, Iceland.

In 750 AD Irish monks were the first settlers in Iceland and built monasteries along the coast followed by a Norse settlement. Ingolfr Arnanson establishes the town of Reykjavik, which means (cozy inlet) describing the geothermal steam. In the year 930 Reykjavik establishes Europe's oldest parliament.

With the sunshine and a temperature of 43 degrees I walked to Old Town and past all the Embassies and found Reykjavik to be a beautiful city. The New Town section has tree-lined streets in front of the modern stores.   An impressive Opera House and Symphony Hall provide a cultural environment supporting the arts.   Iceland has high taxes but all education and medical is free resulting in a healthy intelligent society.

The entire scenic waterfront of Reykjavik is a bike path and walking promenade allowing pedestrians to enjoy the natural scenery. President Regan had his summit meeting with Gorbachov in a building on the waterfront promenade. The United States presented a gift to Iceland of a statue of Leif Erickson proudly on display.

Reykjavik is a world-renowned hot spot for nightlife and young people enjoying bars and restaurants,

GREENLAND

As we approach Greenland we see many ice burgs, some even larger than our ship and of course the tragedy of the Titanic comes to mind. I believe they even showed the movie on board which makes this trip even more eventful. Greenland is the largest island in the world with a population of 45,000 and is a territory of Denmark. Christianity is the chief religion as demanded by King Olaf. Greenland's ice cap is the second largest in the world, second only to Antarctica. Eighty five percent of Greenland is covered by ice cap.

Prince Christian Sound, Greenland

On very limited occasions during about 6 weeks of summer it is sometimes possible for a ship to take a scenic shortcut through Prince Christian Sound. Only about five to ten ships per year pass through this sound. Before our entrance a helicopter verified that the sound was passable.

It was August 31, 2006 and a rare beautiful sunny day as our ship entered the fjords of Prince Christian Sound with cliffs towering over 3800 feet high. The glaciers from the Greenland icecap creating new ice burgs with a great splashes as they fall from the glacier and are born before us in the sound.

The Apostle Mountain and Glacier at 5638 feet comes into view as we enter Ilua Fjord at the base of which is the town of Aappilattog with a population of 160 and the only town on this network of fjords and channels. The residents see so few ships each year that many come to the shoreline to welcome our ship. The M/S Amsterdam blasted the ships horn and whistle and lots of smoke came out of the stack as we passed Aappilattog

The shortcut through Prince Christian Sound and Ilua Fjord saves 66 miles on our way to our next port of Quqortoq. Debbie said this cruise reminded her transit through the Panama Canal where most passengers spent the entire day on deck to view the scenery.   I agreed with her that there is so much to see here in Prince Christian Sound that most everyone is on deck on this beautiful 50-degree day. So far on this North Atlantic crossing Prince Christian Sound is the highlight. A must see for yourself.

Quqortoq, Greenland.

The largest town in Southern Greenland is Quqortoq with a population of 3500. We arrived in the early morning with a dense fog and zero visibility. The ship waited until close to noon for the fog to lift before docking, a reminder of how lucky we were yesterday for the perfect day to transit Prince Christian Sound.

Once the fog lifted we were able to see the many hillside colorful houses of Quqortoq. We saw no trees, yet the houses are all made of wood, prefabricated and shipped here from Denmark in bright colors. Red, blue, green and yellow houses add lots of color to the landscape.

Quqortoc is where Leif Erickson with 35 followers lived over 1000 years ago and traveled from here to Vineland making the first European settlement in North America in the year 999. They called this settlement Vineland when they discovered vines of grapes and berries.

Leif returned to Greenland with lumber and berries and grapes and amazed the population.

CANADA

St. Anthony, Newfoundland, Canada

Leif's father Eric the Red died and Leif took over his responsibilities. Leif's younger brother returned to Vineland in 1004 and traveled further inland where he saw a tepee with 3 canoes and 9 savages hiding beneath. After attacks, Leif's brother died leaving a widow in Greenland. His widow married an Icelander and returned to Vineland to bring back her husbands body.

Three ships left Greenland with 250 men and women to settle in Vineland at sites north of St. Anthony as well as south on the St. Lawrence Estuary. The natives wanted iron weapons and after 3 winters 160 men and 90 women returned to Greenland in 1023

L'Anse aux Meadows, Newfoundland, Canada

The Vikings and Norsemen were illiterate, so there is little documentation; however the evidence is here for everyone to see. Twenty miles north of

St. Vincent is the UNESCO World Heritage site of L'Anse aux Meadows containing the hard evidence needed for proof that a settlement existed here in America as early as the year 999. On this site is the settlement of a furnace and smithy and seven buildings covered over with soil to preserve the settlement that archeologists have determined is the original Leif Erickson site.

St. John's, Newfoundland, Canada

A beautiful natural harbor through a narrow passage with cliffs on both sides is St. John's, Newfoundland's largest city of 200,000.

Walking along Water Street was quite a thrill as Newfoundland always seemed so far away and my Canadian friends joke about their endurance. Well it just like most Canadian or American cities and a pleasure to visit. With this visit to Newfoundland I have been in all the Canadian Provinces except Manitoba and Saskatuan that Debbie and I probably should have visited at the same time I visited North and South Dakota. Poor planning!

New York Harbor, NY

Entering New York Harbor and greeted by the Statue of Liberty puts an end to our Grand Tour of Europe. We are already talking about a World Cruise for January 2007 and have already verified 35 days of it on Oceania Nautica with a dock in every port. Debbie and I learned a lot on this four-month trip concentrating on Europe and the European explorers and look forward to exploring next, the rest of the world.

One of three preserved Viking Ships, Oslo Norway

Glacier, Prince Christian Sound, Greenland

Barbeque on board HAL Amsterdam. Greenland

Quqortoc, Greenland

Ruins of 999 Vinland Settlement

Evidence of Vineland settlement 999 discovered in 1960s

Vinland Settlement L'Anse aux Meadows discovered in Newfoundland

Replica, Norseman Kitchen, L'Anse aux Meadows, Newfoundland

CHAPTER XV

THE SOUTH PACIFIC
CUNARD, QUEEN ELIZABETH 2

We embarked in January 2007 on the Cunard Line; Queen Elizabeth 2 in Los Angeles, CA bound for Sydney, Australia on our first leg of a Round the World Cruise.

San Francisco, CA

Debbie and I have been to San Francisco often, sometimes for a week at a time, but entering San Francisco by ship was a new experience for us, especially on the QE2 going under the Golden Gate Bridge and passing so close to Alcatraz on our way to the pier that is within walking distance to Fisherman's Wharf and trolley access to the entire city.

Honolulu, Hawaii.

Both of us have been to Hawaii before and this time we wanted to see something new, so we hired a cab to take us to Kahala Resort that is North of Diamond head. We spent the day lounging around Kahala and enjoying the turquoise water.

Lahania, Maui, Hawaii.

Nineteenth Century Whaling Community that today has become a laid back quiet tourist part of Hawaii. There are lots of condos and time-shares, as well as beautiful hotels that we had to bypass because of high surf and no dock.

Crossing the Equator.

This is our second time crossing the Equator the last time we were pollywogs crossing from the North Atlantic to the South Atlantic Ocean, on our way to Rio de Janeiro, Brazil. This time we are Shellbacks called to witness the initiation of pollywogs as we cross from the North Pacific to the South Pacific Ocean.

Ships crossing the Equator since 1393 initiated pollywogs (first time crossings) by a ceremony with King Neptune presiding over humiliating ordeals for the entertainment of shellbacks. For example, well-dressed pollywogs have spaghetti poured over them and are thrown into the ships pool. The idea was to welcome pollywogs into the realm of shellbacks, or seasoned sailors. A fun day nevertheless.

FRENCH POLYNESIA

In 1994 Debbie and I visited five islands in French Polynesia, Tahiti, Bora Bora, Huahine, Moorea and Raiatea. This time, however, in comfort on the QE2.

Tahiti,

We dock in Papeete, Tahiti and disembark with a wheelchair. Along the waterfront of Papeete the Tahitians have made a good effort to make it wheelchair friendly, which I did not remember from our last trip. We visited the market and many shops along the waterfront. More work is still needed on the interior sidewalks a few blocks from the waterfront so that business can benefit from wheelchair customers.

Moorea

Probably one of the most beautiful Islands on this planet. Moorea's spectacular jagged mountains appear to have been pushed up out of the sea by a cataclysmic event perhaps eons ago. The scenery inspired filmmakers to film part of South Pacific on this Island with such songs as *Bali Hai*, and *Some Enchanted Evening*. Parts of the recent Mutiny on the Bounty were also filmed here.

TONGA

Tonga has a King and is an independent country, governed by a Constitutional Monarchy. By comparison to Moorea, Tonga is a flat island about the size of the state of New Jersey.

We disembarked in Nuka Alofa the capital city, which has many embassy buildings, but the King's Palace commands the waterfront, with a beautiful park running the length of the harbor. The Palace is of Victorian architecture and constructed of wood, prefabricated in New Zealand, shipped to Tonga and reconstructed in 1867 where it has served since as the King's Palace.

Locals talk about the King being visible often, such as having coffee in town with residents.

FIJI

Arriving in the harbor of Suva, Fiji's capital, the QE2 docks and we go ashore to find great efforts to make the city wheelchair friendly. It is evident in Fiji that progress is being made to attract disabled visitors.

Fiji's islands spread across the Koro Sea. If you are invited to dinner, be careful that you are not served as dinner. Cannibalism existed in some of these 322 Fiji islands until 1920.

Kahala Resort,Oahu, Hawaii

The point, Kalaha Resort, Hawaii

Papeete, Tahiti, French Polynesia

Moorea, French Polynesia

The QE2 off the coast of Moorea, French Polynesia

CHAPTER XVI

NEW ZEALAND

New Zealand.

Discovered by the Dutchman Abel van Tasman in 1642 and named Niuew Zeeland, Abel van Tasman was discouraged from exploring further by cannibals who dined on members of his crew.

Captain James Cook the British Explorer sailed on the Endeavor in 1769 around the two large islands of New Zealand and mapped and claimed the land for Britain. The islands were populated with Maori thought to be descendants of Polynesians.

Progressing from a British Colony in 1856 to a Dominion in 1907 to finally in 1947 the independent country of New Zealand, as we know it today, New Zealand is fascinating..

New Zealand has something for everyone, from skiing to sailing. In fact, New Zealand, a sailor's paradise, has more sailors per capita than anywhere on the face of the earth. New Zealander's have even won the prestigious America's Cup. The people have an environmental conscience so New Zealand is clean and green. New Zealand consists of two large islands and quite a few smaller islands some uninhabited. Surprisingly the country is larger than the UK although not as populated. An environmental spirit for a pristine country dominates the population as Debbie and I noticed visiting three of its largest cities.

AUCKLAND

At home in San Diego, we often have lunch in the oldest tavern in San Diego called the Waterfront that is owned by our dear friend Nancy Nichols. Our ship docked in beautiful Auckland Harbor and as we walked off the pier Debbie spotted Auckland's Waterfront Restaurant.

"Let's take a picture for Nancy," she asked?

"Sure, let's have lunch there as well," I responded.

It was still too early for a restaurant so I pushed Debbie in her wheelchair along Queen Street in the heart of downtown. At one point we had to stop for hundreds and hundreds of motorcycles with police escort were coming down the hill on Queen Street. Pedestrians on the sidewalk waited more than 20 minutes to cross the street for this motorcycle rally to pass. A local couple pushing a stroller parked next to the wheelchair and explained amid the roar of the cycles that the rally is an annual event and riders from all parts of New Zealand come to participate. The little boy in the stroller was covering his ears and laughing. Quite exciting and we were happy to see it

With the passing of the last motorcycle, those waiting to cross the street, did so and we resumed out walk up the hill along Queen Street, passing many shops, restaurants and galleries until we got even with the giant tower and turned around to go back down the hill.

By now the Waterfront restaurant was opened. To our surprise it was completely wheelchair accessible, even to the point of getting a table at the water's edge. Sunday Brunch is a favorite in Nancy's Waterfront

Restaurant and so it is here in Auckland's Waterfront. We had a wonderful brunch and took many photos to bring home to Nancy.

Before returning to the ship we walked to the Maritime Museum that has an America's Cup Yacht on display and on to the Ferry Terminal where so many locals were boarding different ferries to visit islands off Auckland. Some of the islands have beautiful beaches that attract crowds on such a beautiful day.

WELLINGTON

Wellington is located on the southern tip of North Island so it is very close to South Island across the Cook Straight making it an ideal centralized capital of New Zealand

The capital of New Zealand contains the Parliament Buildings that are set in a beautiful park and are quite distinctive, especially the Beehive. The Beehive, looks like a beehive and was designed by Sir Basil Spence, a British Architect. The construction took 11 years and it was finally completed in 1980.

From a photographic point of view, taking photos of the Beehive is a must as it is quite unique.

CHRISTCHURCH

One of the early settlers was educated at Christ Church College at Oxford, thus the namesake of this appealing city that incorporated in 1862.

Cathedral Square marks the center of town that can't be missed as a tall English style gothic cathedral dominating the south end of the square at the intersection of Comombo Street and Worcester Street. We approached the cathedral from the Botanic Gardens at the foot of

Worcester Street and as we walked toward it there were many booths participating in a weekend farmers market. There were hundreds of people using the square as a park to relax and enjoy the festivities on this beautiful day. Later we walked about 10 blocks down Colombo Street looking for a supermarket that we eventually found.

Auckland, Wellington and Christchurch are beautiful places and each city has a concern for the disabled. Traffic lights designed to assist the blind, sidewalks that enable wheel chair access make these three cities a delight for those needing a wheelchair.

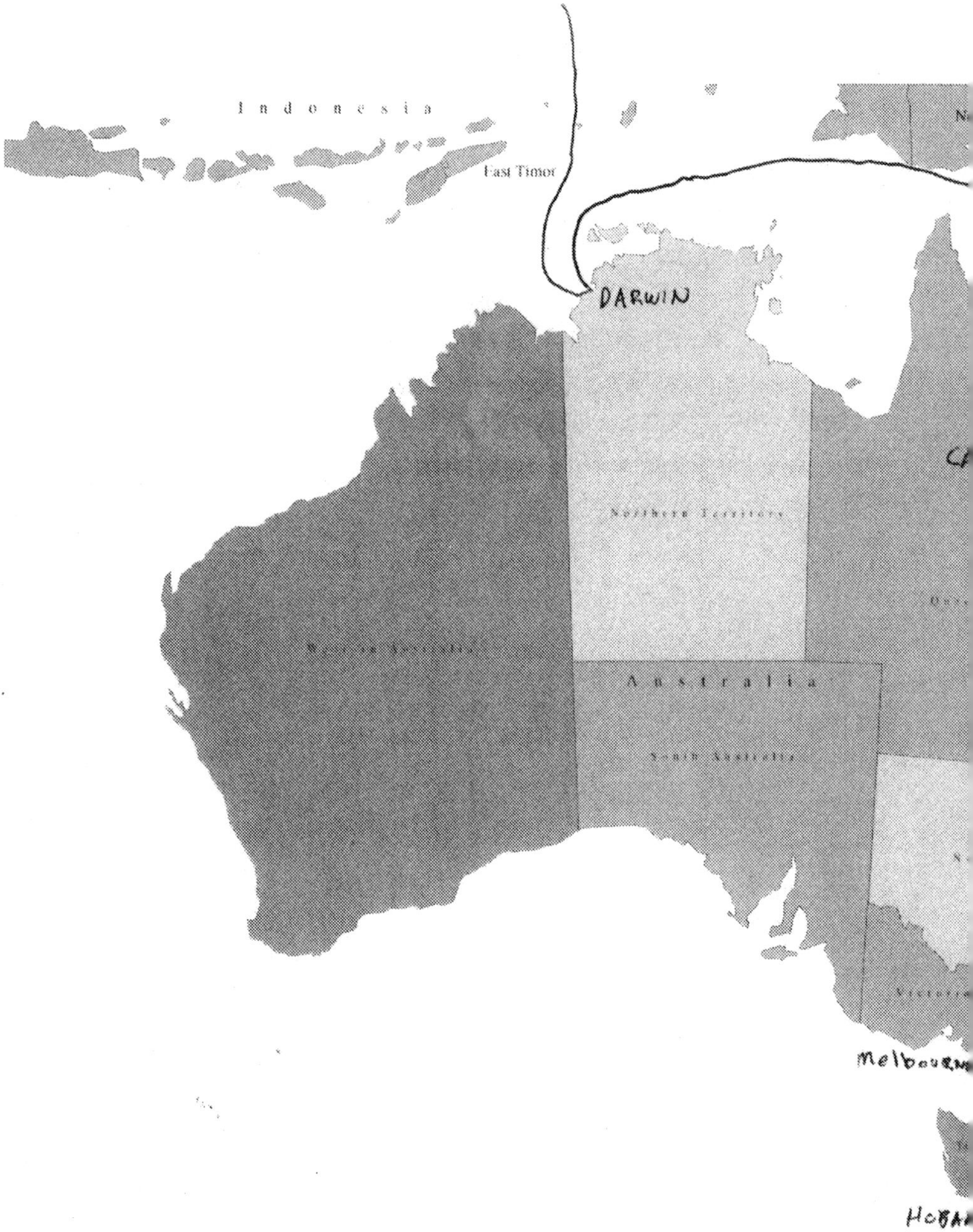

Indonesia

East Timor

DARWIN

Northern Territory

Australia

Western Australia

South Australia

Victoria

MELBOURNE

HOBART

Papua
New Guinea

Solomon
Islands

CAIRNS

WHITSUNDAY
ISLANDS

Vanuatu

New Caledonia

BRISBANE

MV STATENDAM

HMS QUEEN ELIZABETH 2

New South Wales

Sydney

New Zealand

RT

Beehive, Wellington, New Zealand

Town Square, Christchurch, New Zealand

Leaving Christchurch, escort boat and QE2 salute each other

Leaving New Zealand, bound for Australia

CHAPTER XVII

AUSTRALIA

Australia is a continent as well as a country and is the approximate size of the continental United States and is close to the size of Europe. The country is divided into seven large states and the Australian Capital Territory containing the Capital City, Canberra. We plan on visiting five of the seven states on this trip recognizing so many similarities with the United States such as its 1620 settlement by pilgrims seeking Religious Freedom and convicts deported to Australia to commence settlement in 1788.

Both Australia and the United States had a gold rush that helped increase the population in remote areas. Both countries were participants in the World Wars and both are Democracies and today recognize the equal rights of Aborigines and Native Americans.

So then the parallel growth in both time and development of both countries make our mate in the Southern Hemisphere a wonderful and friendly place to visit.

G'day mate!

TASMANIA

This Island off the Southeastern coast of Australia started as a penal colony and eventually became a state in 1853 when its prisoners were freed. Hobart, with its natural harbor, said to be the deepest harbor in the World became the capital of Tasmania.

Hobart.

Today, Hobart is Australia's southernmost major city with a population of 200,000 Georgian and Victorian architecture abound as we walk around this beautiful city. We were fortunate to arrive in Tasmania on a sunny Saturday when Hobart has its giant market open until 3:00 pm at Salamanca Place. Thousands of Tasmanians, "Tassies", shop at the hundreds of booths and frequent the bars and restaurants at Salamanca Place.

Tasmania, is known for its spectacular scenery, National Parks and outdoor activities like hiking, camping, sailing, cycling etc.

VICTORIA

Melbourne, Australia

Melbourne, in the state of Victoria and is the second largest city in Australia. With only a single day here, it is difficult to really come to conclusions, except to say Melbourne is very modern city with a tram that allows you to get from the pier to the heart of the city and visit the shops on Collins Street and Elizabeth Street. A very clean modern city.

NEW SOUTH WALES

Sydney, Australia

Little did we realize the most amazing day that awaited us as the QE2 approached Sydney Harbor on February 20, 2007? It has been 65 years since the original Cunard Queen Mary and Queen Elizabeth both used as troop ships in World War II met in Sydney Harbor in 1942.

By mid-afternoon, private yachts and boats of all sizes came out of the harbor to greet Cunard Line's QE2 as it approached Sydney Harbor, led by a fire boat shooting water high in the air in three directions to join the QM2 already docked on the Quay.

As the ship approached the Queen Mary 2 already docked accompanied by a flotilla of hundreds upon hundreds of small craft and sightseeing boats we could see the many thousands of spectators on shore waving and cheering as the two Queens saluted each other with a defining tremendous three blasts from their stacks. The sight was so uplifting and emotional that many around us on deck were in tears on the QE2 while still others on deck were waving and cheering to the spectators on shore.

As the QE2 continued toward the two famous landmarks of the Harbor Bridge and the Sydney Opera House, the flotilla accompanying the ship was diverted toward the bridge while the QE2 turned to port side after passing the Opera house very close where those aboard admired this architectural achievement from every angle.

The QE2 eventually docked starboard to the Sydney Cruise Ship Terminal and by 9:00 pm with crowds on deck on both the QE2 and QM2 on the other side of the opera house and the thousands of spectators on shore in between and around the harbor started cheering the first burst of fireworks as they flashed over the Sydney Opera House. With the QE2 and QM2 berthed on the far shore on opposite sides of the Opera House and the flotilla of yachts and small craft throughout the harbor, it was quite an exhilarating scene, topped off by a tremendous fireworks display to celebrate the arrival of the Queen Mary 2 on its Maiden Voyage World Cruise and Queen Elizabeth 2, Silver Jubilee 25th World Cruise. This was not only a historic day for Cunard Cruise Lines but also an exciting day that will remain with Debbie and me forever.

Waitera, our home base for Sydney.

Fortunately we stayed on the ship after the fireworks and did not have to join the gridlock traffic jam caused by the huge crowd all wanting to leave the harbor after the fireworks. The next morning we left for Waitera, a Sydney suburb where we stayed for nine days in Waldorf Apartments, a time-share complex complete with an equipped kitchen, living room and beautiful large covered deck overlooking lush gardens.

Last year we used Oravieto Italy as our home base for Rome. This year Waitara for a home base for Sydney, only 45 minutes by train to the harbor. A local couple asked: "Why did you pick this place?" I smiled and said, "To meet people just like you."

The first two days were spent exploring that which is in walking distance around Waitara. We found only three blocks away the Westfield Shopping Mall of which there are many in San Diego, but this we were told this is Westfield's first ever Shopping Mall.

Sydney Opera House.

With Opera Tickets in hand and the Waitara Train Station only one large block away, it was off to Sydney by train to the baroque opera *Alcina*, written in 1516 by George Frederic Handle. What a contrast, a baroque opera performed in such a marvel of modern architecture, the Sydney Opera House.

Handel's *Messiah, Water Music and Royal Fireworks* were all familiar to us but not his operas, so Alcina was an enjoyable musical experience that relates well to Handel's other works.

The Sydney Opera House really does captivate ones imagination. We have visited opera houses that are considered modern in the US such as Lincoln Center in New York City and the Dorothy Chandler Pavilion in Los Angeles; both have separate buildings across a square for the Symphony Hall and Opera House. The same is true for Helsinki, Finland with its modern new opera house nearby its symphony hall.

The Premier of New South Wales, in 1956 announced a competition to design an opera house for Sydney, Australia. Danish architect Jorn Utzon won the competition from more than 200 entries from around the world. In Jorn Utzon"s own words as expressed in his writing the Forward to the book *Building a Masterpiece: The Sydney Opera House;* "The sensation I felt when it was announced that my scheme had been selected for first prize was one of elation beyond comparison. The next many, busy years expanded my world and developed me as an architect in a way that nothing else could have done."

Unlike so many modern opera houses like the Metropolitan Opera house in Lincoln Center, New York, or the Dorothy Chandler Pavilion in Los Angeles, Jorn Utzon has combined the Concert hall, Opera Theatre, restaurants, bars, Drama Theatre under one magnificent roof suggesting billowing sails at Bennelong Point jutting out into Sydney Harbor below and complementing the landmark Sydney Harbor Bridge.

Our nine days of condo living in a suburb of Sydney were coming to an end as we took a cab to the Sydney Cruise Ship terminal to board the Holland America, MS Statendam destined for additional ports of call in Australia and the Orient.

The company's first ship was the Rotterdam that sailed on its maiden voyage from the Netherlands to New York City in 1872. A year later the official name Holland America Lines was adopted as they commenced operations in Hoboken, NJ. The popular "dam" suffix for each ship has been a tradition of Holland America ever since. By their 25th Anniversary in 1898 they owned six ships all ending in 'dam" that carried 490,000 passengers and became a major carrier of immigrants to America from Europe. Last year we sailed on the MS Amsterdam from St. Petersburg Russia to New York and this year on the Statendam from Sydney to Dalian, China and on Rotterdam VI from Monaco to London and we are already scheduled to circumnavigate South America on the Princeindam in 2008. Damn good ships, all wheelchair accessible with interesting itineraries. At the time of this writing Holland America had 13 modern ships all with names ending with, "dam".

QUEENSLAND

Brisbane, Australia

Brisbane is the third largest city in Australia and is the capital of the state of Queensland. Our ship, the Statendam negotiated the Brisbane River quite a distance before approaching the relatively new Cruise Ship Terminal. Holland America provided a free Shuttle Bus Service to the center of Brisbane by the Queen Street Mall where we walked toward the Brisbane River and about 9:00 am Debbie spotted the Conrad International Treasury Casino.

We did not expect the Queen Street Mall to open until 10:00 so needless to say the Casino was our first stop and we spent two hours playing the slots and left quite happy, because we left as winners, not like our first trip to Casino Monte Carlo in Monaco last spring.

From the casino we crossed the Victoria bridge to the Cultural Center, where the Queensland Performing Center offers Opera, Classical Music, Ballet as well as theatrical productions in very modern facilities. Their Museums of Art and Natural History are also located nearby in the Cultural Center.

Brisbane is very easy to walk around as streets are named for Kings, Queens, Prince and Princess with male names running east-west and females north-south, so our return shuttle to the ship will be on the corner of Elizabeth and Albert Streets.

Whitsunday Islands, Queensland, Australia

Of the 74 Islands comprising the Whitsundays, most are uninhabited, yet a few islands are home to spectacular resorts. Our ship took us to Hamilton Island a well-groomed island full of tropical plants, pristine beaches and five star resorts.

The islands got this unusual name when Captain Cook reached the Islands in 1770 on Whit Sunday (7th Sunday after Easter), thus the name Whitsunday Islands.

It is not often you find free shuttle service throughout an Island. Hamilton Island has the Green, Purple and Orange Shuttles. The Beaches are spectacular. Hamilton has a large marina that is also a departure point for the Great Barrier Reef.

The Great Barrier Reef, Queensland, Australia.

One of the Natural Wonders of the World, the Great Barrier Reef attracts scuba divers, snorkels, and swimmers from around the world to view the more than 2000 species of fish and tropical marine life in their natural environment. The reef is more than 1000 miles long and is made up of more than 2500 separate reefs, supporting more than 30,000 thousand species. The Great barrier is the largest living organism on the earth and joins the Great Wall of China as easily visible from outer space.

Cairns, Queensland, Australia

Cairns, pronounced KANZ is a beautiful city in Northern Queensland and serves as still another embarkation port for accessing the Great Barrier Reef. Our ship, the Statendam after sailing the Coral Sea entered a narrow channel as we approached Cairns. The city became larger and larger until we docked Trinity Pier within a block of all the downtown shopping and a few blocks from the beautiful Esplande Park along the waterfront.

Our first stop was the Great Barrier Reef Hotel, a landmark hotel built in the late 1800s. It was the architecture that attracted us, as we sat below a covered roof in their outdoor café to make cell phone calls to the United States. Debbie of course spotted the Casino at the Sofitel Hotel a block away, so we made it our destiny to lose some of the money we won in the Whitsunday Islands, just the day before.

Quantas Airlines was founded nearby in the small town of Cloncurry and is an acronym for Queensland and Northern Territory Air Service that started in 1928 by Reverend John Flynn. His service is honored in the Royal Flying Doctor Base near the beautiful Flecker Botanical Gardens.

The climate in Cairns is tropical, but our day here had a constant breeze that made our walk around the city a very pleasant one. There is so much to see in Cairns, that one day is not enough, we had to forego the sky ride over the rainforest, the Karunda Scenic Trail, a vintage train ride past gorges, waterfalls and through a rainforest and the Green and Fitzroy Islands where snorkeling on the Great barrier Reef can be accomplished without the danger of jellyfish.

NORTHERN TERRATORY

The main towns of the Northern Territory are Darwin on the lush North Coast and Alice Springs in the arid center. The Northern Territory has not yet achieved statehood due to its small population, the territory however, is self governed since 1978. Alice Springs is a small town near the huge red Uluru, Ayers Rock, which with our day in the Northern Territory was impractical for us to visit on this trip.

Darwin, Australia.

Darwin was named in 1839 for Charles Darwin by John Stokes, Captain of the ship HMS Beagle a full 20 years before the published book, The Origin of the Species, in honor of their friendship as naturalist and captain.

Darwin, on the North Coast of the Northern Territory has a tropical climate containing an unusually large collection of plants, reptiles, birds and mammals and is home to one of the oldest races of man, the Aborigines.

The Japanese in there attempt to dominate the South Pacific, bombed Darwin 64 times and it wasn't until the Americans came to Australia's aid in the Battle of the Coral Sea off the coast of Queensland where Japan lost their first ship, the sinking of light carrier Shoho. The American's lost their carrier Lexington but damaged two other Japanese Aircraft Carriers that withdrew from the battle for repairs and were not able to be used in the decisive battle of Midway.

With the loss of 21 out of 27 aircraft and some of their best trained pilots, Japan learned that their Navy was not invincible, yet they claimed a victory in the Battle of the Coral Sea, having sunk the Lexington and severely damaged the Yorktown, before withdrawing.

To the amazement of the Japanese the damaged Yorktown was repaired in a matter of 36 hours in Hawaii and was joined at Midway by the carrier Hornet, thought to be in the Atlantic and too wide for the Panama Canal. Midway of course was a decisive American victory and the turning point of the war in the Pacific while the Battle of the Coral Sea protected Australia from invasion and Japanese occupation.

On Christmas Eve, 1974 cyclone Tracy with 175 mph winds leveled the city of Darwin. With only a few buildings remaining, the next morning started Australia's largest evacuation with 66 dead and upwards of 30,000 people removed by aircraft while reconstruction of the city began.

Today Darwin is a very modern city, with very few old buildings. The new Darwin contains buildings designed to withstand future cyclones. Citizens of Darwin welcome Americans and freely discuss the battle of the Coral Sea.

QE2 joins QM2 in Sydney, Thousands cheering on shore

Sydney Opera House, Sydney, Australia

Flotilla to welcome QE2 enter Sydney harbor

Fireboat turns at bridge, Sydney, Australia

CHAPTER XVIII

INDONESIA

It is with 130 active volcanoes and 13,670 islands that make up this fertile country of Indonesia. Bali the small island most famous because of its natural beauty, splendid beaches and terraced rice patties is part of the Indonesian chain of larger islands of which Borneo, Java and Sumatra are the largest. These islands were previously called the Spice Islands for their rare spices that could preserve meat such as pepper, cloves and cinnamon that were in great demand in Europe. The Dutch eventually cornered the market on spices and changed the name to Dutch East Indies. 231,000,000 people populate this archipelago.

Bali, Indonesia

Once past the gauntlet of welcoming Balinese trying to sell you a shirt, woodcarvings or postcards, and countless souvenirs, a cab was located for a trip to Ubeu.

Java, Indonesia

Samarang is the capital city of Java with 2,000,000 people and is located on the north coast of the island. Highlights of Samarang include the busy harbor, the Dutch colonial homes and warehouses of the old town built during the Dutch occupation. Islam is the primary religion.

A magnificent temple on the island of Java is Borobudor, built in the 8th and 9th centuries on the Kedu Plain near Yogyakarta by five generations of workers numbering in the thousands and should not be missed. Second only to Angkor Wat in Cambodia Borobudor is an impressive UNESCO World Heritage Site, and an architectural achievement containing the world's largest carved stone stupa.

Bali Temple, Bali, Indonesia

CHAPTER XIX

REPUBLIC OF SINGAPORE

Singapore

Stamford Raffles recognizing this strategic importance of this island of about 1000 inhabitants founded Singapore in 1819 and claimed it for the British East India Company. Today this island nation is one of the most densely populated cities in the world and contains a blend of cultures from Chinese, Malay, Hindu and English reflecting its colonial past.

Debbie and I visited the Arab Section and enjoyed the Sultan Mosque and spent some time in Chinatown with its Buddhist Temple and Tea Houses and shopped in the narrow alleys for bargains before heading out to Little India to the beautiful Hindu Temple. These three sections of the city represent the three largest populations who live in peaceful harmony with each other.

The world famous Raffles Hotel, frequented by such authors as Rudyard Kipling, Somerset Maughm and now yours truly as well as celebrities Charlie Chaplin and Noel Coward insure that the list goes on. In Raffles Hotel you can sit in a large wicker chair and dine on gourmet food or visit Raffles Long Bar for a Singapore Sling and throw peanut shells on the floor and not have it considered the crime of littering.

Orchard Road can lead you to the Botanical Gardens and is lined with luxury shops and hotels and is a place where tourists enjoy the malls.

On our World Cruise we are fortunate to visit Singapore twice, once on MS Statendam and once on MS Nautica. Each visit is memorable as Singapore is so clean; there is no graffiti, no littering and little or no crime by residents. There is so much Americans can learn from this peaceful law abiding society with harsh penalties for misdemeanors.

On the banks of the Singapore River locals and tourists join together at Clark Quay and Boat Quay exploring the many shops, restaurants and bars. Some establishments offer music and others evening entertainment.

Lee Kuan Yew in 1959 became prime minister of the Republic of Singapore and served until 1990. Singapore has grown to 4.6 million people.

The Singapore River Boat Tour is a great way to see the city.

Views from Mt. Faber by funicular or Santosa Island are photo opportunities.

Raffel's Hotel, Singapore

Singapore Sling at Raffel's Hotel Singapore

CHAPTER XX

CHINA

Xiamen, China

Pronounced, J-men or Z-men, Xiamen is the city where Chang Ki Chek and the Nationalist Chinese left for the island of Formosa off the coast of Xiamen. The park in the city honors Dr. Sun-yat Sen, the revolutionary hero of 1911. After a visit to the bustling modern city a ferry ride to the island of Gu Lang-Yu is a wonderful experience in a beautiful manicured park like setting.

Indoor and outdoor markets provide an interesting shopping experience, complete with the many different odors of fresh fish, fruits and vegetables all in a centralized area with the skyline of Xiamen on the opposite shore. The island is small, about 1½ square miles and there are very few vehicles so walking is encouraged. The trails throughout the island are well maintained and artistically designed to compliment the beautiful gardens that appear at many turns. The southern tip of the island at the Bright Moon Garden is the statue of Zheng Chenggong, who defended the last Ming Emperor before the downfall of the dynasty.

Shanghai, China

There are those who claim the Twenty-first Century will belong to China. It is our visit to Shanghai and Hong Kong that provides insight into this possibility. The two cities are competitive in trying to attract the most business. Shanghai with an excess of 13,000,000 people is absolutely booming and has become the largest city in China. There are cranes everywhere building new skyscrapers on both sides of the Huangpu River that divides the city.

The west side of the Huangpu River was developed by the British in the 1840s during this colonial era foreigners had concessions from China called extra-territoriality to operate under their respective laws rather than the laws of China. The Opium Wars during this period insured the balance of trade favored the English and left Britain controlling both Hong Kong and Shanghai. The Bund, a beautiful Park along the riverbank on the western side of the river was accented by rows of impressive buildings from this colonial era where major business deals were made. The Peace Hotel overlooking the river a landmark from this era of foreign control where the local population got poorer and poorer and the British, Americans and French prospered.

One hundred years later in the 1940s foreigners gave up their unusual trade status in the face of growing Chinese opposition. In 1949 Chen Yi became the first mayor of Shanghai and his monument stands before the Peace Hotel in the Bund.

Across the river is the Pudong section of Shanghai that was once a slum and is today a marvel of exceptional architecture with corporate identities gracing so many new buildings and continuing construction everywhere. Corporations serious about international business really need a visible presence in Shanghai among these corporate giants.

The Pearl TV tower easily recognizable is the third largest structure of its kind in the world, behind Toronto and Russia's towers.

Beijing, China

Beijing, the capital city of The People's Republic of China is about 24 miles inland from its seaport Tianjin (Xingang). Our ship arrived in Tianjin in dense fog that later turned to rain at 43 degrees. Not a very nice day to visit the Great Wall of China built between 220 and 210 BC or even the main attractions in Beijing such as Tiananmen Square, the worlds largest public square built during the Ming Dynansty. The Forbidden City completed in 1420 in the center of Beijing, with its Imperial Garden, Halls of harmony and temples and palaces will have to wait for a nice day before we venture out to these sights in the cold rain. Fortunately, we are in port for two days and hope for sunshine tomorrow.

Dalian, China

Dalian once part of Manchuria and occupied by the Japanese until the end of World War II when it was turned over to Russia. Russia benefited from Dalian's deep harbor and better climate allowing the port to remain open all year while the Russian Port of Vladavastok is often closed each year by ice.

The architecture of this city shows both a Russian and Japanese influence that although belonging to China today will be preserved as part of Dalian's history.

Dalian is our destination port to disembark Holland America's Statendam, get a taxi to Dalian Airport and fly Air China to Hong Kong, to board the ship Oceana, Nautica for a thirty-five day cruise to the Mediterranean. As much as we avoid airline travel this 3-½ hour non-stop flight we tolerated as a necessity.

Hong Kong, China

Hong Kong has made many efforts to make their city wheelchair accessible but blew it big time on the Ocean Terminal in Kowloon.

Our ship docked at the Ocean Terminal in Kowloon, said to be extremely modern with a shopping mall so large there is no need to go elsewhere. Our impression differs. Although there are many high-end stores in this mall, whoever designed the project should be held accountable for the nightmare of stairs created and a redesign is certainly in order.

Wheelchair friendly cruise ships deliver passengers on a level gangway to a level promenade at the terminal. The promenade leads to an entryway into the terminal with six unnecessary wide steps down into the terminal. A ramp along side the steps is certainly possible. Instead the infamous Rube Goldberg wheelchair lift awaits the disabled person. This device makes a spectacle of the disabled person by stopping pedestrian traffic. Once in the terminal steps are everywhere, elevators do not serve the mall with any efficiency. If you take an elevator to the third floor, you still encounter steps without handrails on the third floor with the ubiquitous wheel chair lift to the right or left of the very wide staircase. It took us a very long time to even find an elevator that goes to the third floor as elevators are marked G, 1, 2, 5, 6, 7 etc., others marked with other random floors.

Within a few feet of leaving the elevator, once again we encounter another very wide staircase with 6 steps still on the third floor. You are supposed to push the red button on the wheelchair lift to have an attendant arrive and operate this monstrosity. After a five minute wait the attendant shows up with his key, puts the safety bars in place with a loud clang and with a lot of fanfare puts Debbie in her wheelchair on the lift and starts the machine with crowds now gapping at all this fanfare for just six steps. Quite dehumanizing! A simple ramp could eliminate this spectacle.

It should be obvious to anyone that the design of this mall and terminal is to maximize rental space without regard for the disabled. To fix the problem, ramps should be installed adjacent to each staircase that could encroach on the entryway to a mall storefront as steps go straight down and ramps are graded down taking slightly more space. Another solution is a small elevator that goes straight down a depth of 6 steps.

It should be obvious to everyone, that the Ocean Terminal In Kowloon was sold a bill of goods when complicated and unfriendly Rube Goldberg wheelchair lifts were installed rather that simple ramps or a more expensive wheelchair elevator. Throughout the terminal and mall there are too many staircases as if steps are okay if a wheel chair lifts are installed adjacent. Someone actually bought this bad idea.

Disabled cruise ship passengers should be aware of this modern, unsympathetic terminal and request the cruise line to boycott this terminal until ramps are installed.

The cruise ships throughout the Industry do a wonderful job of retrofitting older ships to accommodate the disabled and the design of new ships take mobility disabilities into account. Cruise lines should therefore recommend a redesign of the Ocean Terminal in Kowloon, to at least match what the ships provide disabled passengers and if no attempt is made to correct this hideous treatment of the disabled passengers, ships should avoid the terminal completely by choosing a more user friendly terminal.

Kowloon itself is a wonderful wheelchair friendly city. Once out of Ocean Terminal in Kowloon, walking along Canton Street is a wonderful introduction to the city. The Sidewalks are wide and wheelchair friendly and the street is lined with some of the most famous name brand stores. The quality of shops compare well with those on Rodeo Drive in the US.

Macou, China

A Portuguese Territory in China given Independence as late as 1999. For those who enjoy Casinos and fancy hotels Macou is just an hour jet boat ride from Hong Kong and a fun place to visit. Debbie and I have frequented Wynn Resort in Las Vegas and being curious about Steve Wynn's new Resort in Macou, just could not resist the temptation to check it out. Travelers need a Passport to visit Macou that is stamped when departing Hong Kong and entering Macou and again, leaving Macou and returning to Hong Kong.

We took New World First Ferry Services Limited from Kowloon to Macou leaving from a modern wheelchair friendly ferry terminal and arrived in Macou Ferry terminal with similar amenities. Both ferry terminals are as modern as new airport terminals complete with carousels for baggage handling and shops galore. Macou harbor has many casinos lining the waterfront with many of them offering free shuttle service to and from Macou Ferry Terminal to the casino.

We had no trouble finding Wynn's free shuttle to the hotel and casino and spent the afternoon at Wynn admiring the Chinese compulsion for gambling. In the US there seems to be more slots than table games. The reverse is true in Macou; those playing table games far outnumber those playing slots. Blackjack and poker are favorites here.

Debbie enjoys the slots and was able to more than double her money on this our first visit to Macou. It was a fun day and nice to leave Macou a winner, embark on the high speed ferry and return to Kowloon.

Macou just adds to our list of World Heritage sights visited.

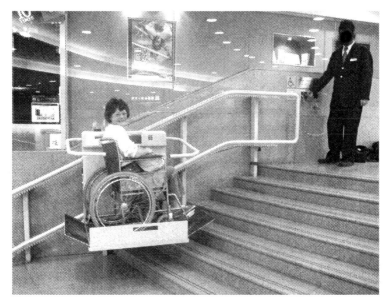

Kowloon Cruise Ship Terminal Rube Goldberg 7 step lift

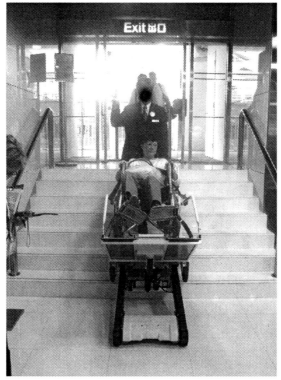

Rube Goldberg 7 step lift

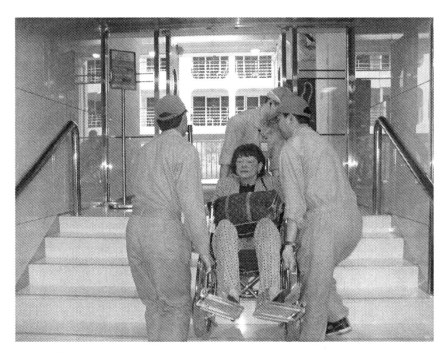

A simple ramp can do it

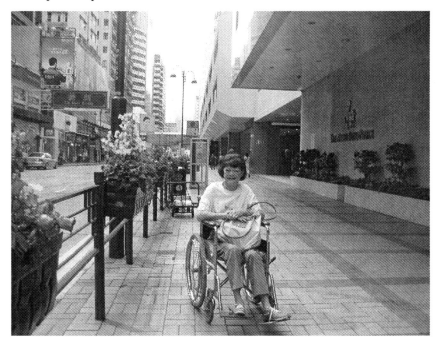

On the wheelchair friendly streets of Kowloon, China

Shanghai Harbor, Shanghai, China

Sculpture, Xiamen, China

CHAPTER XXI

VIETNAM

Da Nang, Vietnam

Gale force winds, rain and zero visibility, closed the port of Da Nang on the day of our visit. By 9:00 am the Captain announced that the ship would commence sailing to Na Trang, Vietnam that we previously visited on the MS Statendam.

Nha Trang, Vietnam

Nha Trang is a resort town in Viet Nam with beautiful beaches, colonial buildings and many tree-lined streets. The Mo Ped is the peoples form of transportation, there are thousands of them zig zaging their way about town. The beach is popular from 5:00 am to 8:00 am before work while they enjoy tai chi, volleyball, swimming and other beach activities. The Vietnamese prefer not to be on the beach with mid-day sun, so the beach is empty most of the day for international travelers.

The guidebooks all mention the Big Buddha with 200 or more steps to negotiate on the mountain. Debbie and I hired a cab for the day and to our surprise the cab driver went up back alleys with garbage cans, buildings with laundry on their balconies and dogs in the narrow passages until right before us we behold the Big Budda without climbing the 200 steps. I took Debbie's photo with Big Buddha.

The Sleeping Buddha provided another sensational photo opportunity. The cab driver took us to the fishing fleet and other sights in Nha Trang and our first visit to Viet Nam was a wonderful day.

Ho Chi Mihn City (Saigon), Vietnam.

After the fall of Saigon in 1975 the communists renamed the city Ho Chi Minh City after its socialist founder. Saigon is still a name preferred by many of its six million citizens, many on motorbikes. They move too fast to count and crossing the street in Saigon can be tedious.

The French colonized and occupied Vietnam in 1859. Wide tree-lined boulevards of Saigon show the French influence throughout the city. Sidewalk cafes and French Architecture abound and many citizens continue to speak French. The French withdrew from Vietnam in 1954 after the battle of Dien Bien Phu and the country became separated into North and South Vietnam and stayed that way until reunification in 1976.

The rice crop of the South has three planting seasons compared to one planting season in the North. The entire country is shaped like the letter S with Ho Chi Mihn City, the financial center in the south on the Saigon River.

Our ship entered the Saigon River from the South China Sea at the Makong Delta. Traveling upriver to Ho Chi Mihn City takes a few hours and the scenery is beautiful as the delta region is lush green.

As we sail up the Saigon River we see many wooden fishing boats with Vietnamese fishing the river. Many container ships pass us leaving Saigon Harbor and heading out to sea only increasing our anticipation of what we are about to see in Saigon.

We finally see the skyline of this great city and it grows larger and larger until we are finally docked and disembark.

We head for the corner of Le Loi Blvd. and Nguyen Hue Blvd. and started walking toward the Notre Dame Cathedral of Saigon, built by the French in colonial times. Naturally a prayer was offered in thanks for our safe trip so far. While walking the streets many Vietnamese stop you to sell you something. They want to bargain, even if it is for a small item like 10 postcards for a dollar or a refrigerator magnet.

We are heading toward the Saigon Opera House and there are quite a few streets to cross. Thousands of motorbikes, scooters, mo-peds or whatever are clogging streets. If you are lucky enough to have a street with lights for pedestrians you will find they are obedient and stop for lights.

Many streets have no traffic lights, so it is zig, zag through the motor-bikes to get across. After a few times of close calls, I reasoned out that you trust the population to watch out for you, and to my surprise, they really do. What an interesting discovery, if you are terrified, just wait for a policeman to blow his whistle to stop the traffic while you cross and there are many policeman walking the streets.

Our overall impression of Ho Chi Mien City is that it is a wheelchair friendly city and wonderful place to visit; the scenery just getting there is quite beautiful. The Vietnamese welcome you to their city and want to do business no mater how small or large. There are many large hotels to choose from, some with quite a history, like the Rex Hotel with its roof garden. There are so many great restaurants and shopping in this vibrant city that is often revered to as the Pearl of the Orient.

I am writing this as we are leaving the city on the Saigon River and the Captain has just announced that the ship will list while making some turns in the river so passengers should be aware. Ha! Sounds like fun doesn't it?

Saigon Opera House Sculptures

Living on the Makong River, Vietnam

CHAPTER XXII

THAILAND

Thailand is a country of smiles. When people speak to you it is with a smile. Thailand is a Constitutional Monarchy with a King as head of state and a parliament elected by the people. Prior to 1949 Thailand was known as Siam, when the name was changed to reflect Thai which means free, thus Thailand is land of the Free,

Laem Chabang, Thailand.

A large, modern port city about 2 hours from Bangkok. Container ships are everywhere, and so are car carriers and cruise ships. Laem Chabang is a busy deepwater harbor serving Bangkok's imports and exports.

Bangkok, Thailand

Bangkok is the capital of Thailand and contains a Royal Palace surrounded by a moat 4.3 miles long nearly a half mile distant from the palace with high walls to protect the palace. The Emerald Buddha and the reclining Buddha

With temperatures well over 100 degrees we asked our pal Jerry Blaine who lives in Thailand for advice. Is there something specific that you would like to see in Bangkok?

We thought for a minute and said not really as we have already seen so many temples, although the Royal Palace and Emerald Buddha if it were cooler would be of interest.

Good said Jerry, I think the heat and crowds of Bangkok might be too much for Debbie, so I suggest you go to Pattaya only a half hour by taxi from Laem Chabang. Pattaya is a resort town on the Gulf of Thailand and you will get a breeze off the water. There are quite a few temples in Pattaya and pretty much everything you want in Bangkok you can also find in Pattaya without the crowds.

Pattaya. Thailand.

Beautiful Beaches with high rise buildings across the street from the beach. There are Lots of nice restaurants and a fine resort area only 45 minutes from Laem Chabang. A van holding about nine people for $60.00 will take you from Laem Chabang to Pattaya round trip and those using the van typically share the cost. Our pal Jerry Blaine, born in Seattle, moved to Thailand and lives near Pattaya. Jerry taught us much about Thailand, its living conditions and customs. There are many Europeans and Americans living here as both housing and the cost are low and the climate is attractive.

Phuket, Thailand

Phuket is Thailand's largest island with a mountain range running from North to South. Tourists are attracted to its beautiful beaches.

CHAPTER XXIII

INDIA

Goa, (Mormugao) India

Goa became a state in India in 1987 shortly after a history of Portuguese rule for 450 years. Portuguese influence is everywhere, especially in the many Christian Churches and colonial architecture. Today Goa contains many resorts frequented by Europeans from October to May each year that have discovered its beautiful beaches and temperate climate. The remaining four months are the Monsoon Season that makes Goa so green.

Debbie and I are fortunate to have a dear friend living in Goa planning to meet the ship as we arrive in port. Her name is Meera Chanai; she was born in India and owned the Pannini Restaurant in La Jolla, CA where we first met her. We spent many good years together in La Jolla learning about India, its food, customs and Hinduism. During this period Debbie and I wrote a cookbook and asked Meera to contribute recipes. My favorite was Meera's eggs that are quite unique with cumin, turmeric and tomato. She later returned to India to care for her aging mother.

We only see Meera when she returns to the US occasionally to visit her son and daughter, so we now look forward to visiting Meera in her native country. After all the hugs and kisses of meeting a close friend on the dock she drove us to Panaji, the capital city of Goa about 45 minutes away where Meera owns a beautiful home high on a hill overlooking the sea.

Meera introduced us to her maids and cooks as well as to her houseguests Diane Thomas and her mother both from La Jolla, CA. Dianne was a wonderful help to Debbie while Meera was busy in the Kitchen. It was no surprise to us that when she served brunch that it featured Meera's Eggs that we love so much with an assortment of curries and Portuguese Bread and rolls. There was spicy melon, onion cookies and many giant bottles of cold Kingfisher Beer that we quaffed down so easily. Life is beautiful!

Meera as always is such a wonderful hostess planning for us such a wonderful day and like a tour guide pointing out the many sights on the way to Panajai. We later went shopping for more beer and to our surprise these giant bottles of kingfisher 650ml (a can of beer is 330 ml) were only 1.00 a bottle, so I bought a case of twelve to bring back to share with friends on the ship.

This day went too fast; at 3:30 it was time to leave for the ship. Meera said she will visit us in San Diego in June and July and so did our new acquaintance Dianne Thomas. So you never know what each day will bring.

Mumbai, (Bombay) India.

Sixteen million inhabitants make Mumbai one of the most densely populated cities in the world. We spent a few hours at the Taj Mahal Hotel in the center of the city overlooking the harbor. This hotel has a first class business office where internet service is available.

Meeera Chanai meets us at the ship in Goa, India

Gate, Mumbai, (Bombay) India

CHAPTER XXIV

THE ARABIAN PENINSULA

OMAN

Oman was known in the ancient world in 1500 BC for its frankincense. Camel caravans crossed the desert often to trade frankincense thought to be a valuable as gold for products from Europe, Asia and Egypt

Salalah, Oman

Salalah is one of Oman's major seaports. Located in the Governorate of Dhofar in the Southwest corner of Oman on the Arabian Sea bordering the Republic of Yemen. Salalah has white sand beaches with a backdrop of the Dhofar Mountain Range.

JORDAN

Aqaba, Jordan

Lawrence of Arabia made this city famous and today it is Jordan's Seaport on the Red Sea. We stayed in Aqaba two days and many of the passengers did an overnight trip to Petra to see the façade of El Khaznah, the Treasury of Petra carved into the sandstone cliffs. I thought this trip through the desert would be too much for Debbie so we contented ourselves listening to the stories from our friends on board when they returned from Petra.

Auto, Train and Cruise Ship, comfortable with a wheelchair.

Cruise from Galveston, TX to Rome, Italy on Celebrity, MV Galaxy, 2006.

Auto trip From Rome, Italy to Florence, Reutte, Austria and on to Bavaria 2006.

Auto Trip from Munich, Germany to Salzberg and Vienna, Austria, 2006

Auto Trip after a week in Vienna to Bayreuth, Germany. 2006

Auto Trip from Bayreuth, Germany to Newschwanstein Castle in Bavaria, 2006

Auto Trip from Bavaria to Strasburg, Colmar and Beaunne, France, 2006

Auto trip from Beaunne in Wine Region to Chateau Region, France, 2006

Train trip from Blois France, to Paris France, 2006

Auto trip from Blois, France to Avignon, France, 2006

Auto trip from Avignon, France to Nice, France, 2006

Auto trip after 12 days in Nice to Monaco, Porto Fino and La Spezia, Italy, 2006

Auto trip to Orviato, Assisi and Rome Italy, 2006

Cruise from Athens, Greece to the Black Sea on Oceana, M/S Nautica, 2006

Cruise from Istanbul, Turkey to Venice, Italy on Oceana, M/S Nautica, 2006

Cruise from Venice, Italy to Barcelona, Spain on Oceana, M/S Nautica, 2006

Cruise from Copenhagen, Denmark to St. Petersburg, Russia, MS Amsterdam

Cruise from St. Petersburg Russia to Wanamunde, Germany, MS Amsterdam, 2006

Train trip from Wanamunde Germany to Berlin , Germany, 2006

Cruise from the Baltic Sea to New York City, HAL, MS Amsterdam, 2006

Cruise from Los Angeles, CA to Sydney Australia, Cunard, QE2, 2007

Cruise from Sydney, Australia to Dalian, China, HAL MS Statendam, 2007

Cruise from Hong Kong China to Athens, Greece, Oceana, Nautica, 2007

Auto trip from Piraeus to Delphi, Greece, 2007

Auto trip from Brussels, Belgium to Amsterdam, Netherlands, 2007

Auto trip from Amsterdam to Luxemburg, 2007

Auto trip from Luxemburg to Romantic Road and on to Munich , Germany, 2007

Auto trip from Liechtenstein and Switzerland to Lake Como, Italy, 2007

Auto trip from Como, Italy to Nice, France, for 9 more days, 2007

Cruise from Monaco to Harwich, England, HAL MS Rotterdam 6, 2007

Auto Trip from La Harve, France to Versaille and Paris, France, 2007

Auto trip from Cork, Ireland to Dingle , Ireland, 2007

Auto trip from Dingle, Ireland to Dublin, Ireland, 2007

Cruise from Southampton, England to New York, Cunard, HMS Queen Mary 2

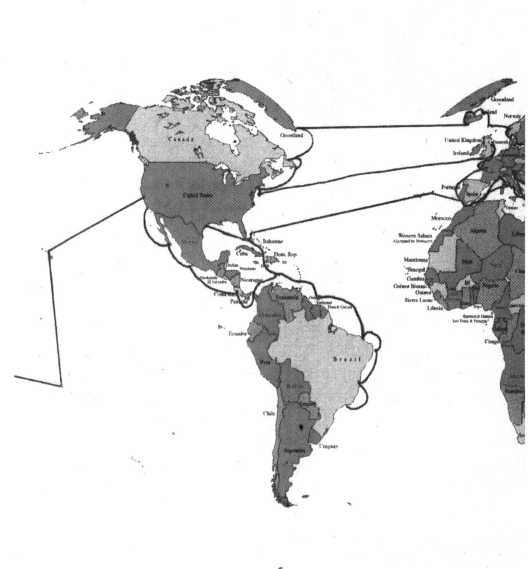

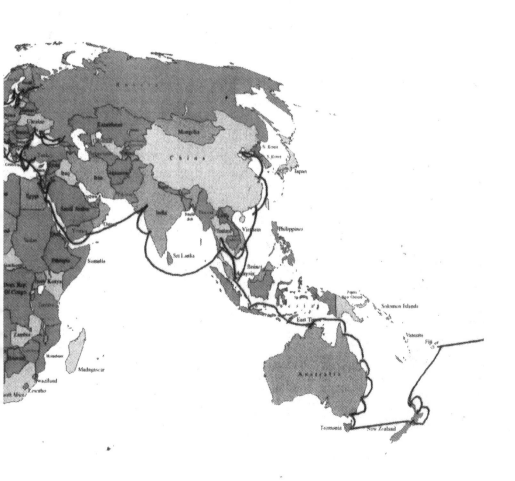

CHAPTER XXV

EGYPT

Debbie and I rarely take escorted tours and prefer a taxi. However, we elected to do so when visiting Egypt as terrorists are potential threat and the tour we took had an armed escort. Better yet, our tour guide Hala who smiled and claimed to be a granddaughter of Queen Neferitti and childless King Tut had a genuine sense of humor complimenting her education as a civil engineer. She called everyone on the tour her Pharaohs and anyone with a question should refer to her as mama Pharaoh

Safaga, Egypt

Safaga is a port city on the Red Sea serving both Hurghada and Luxor. Hurghada is of interest to swimmers and scuba divers looking for crystal clear waters and beautiful beaches on the Red Sea lined with many prominent upscale hotels. Hurghada is about 45 minutes from Safaga by taxi while Luxor is 3 hours and 15 minutes across the mountain range and desert. Bedouins who prefer living in the desert can be seen with herds of goats while others are riding camels and donkeys in the desert. The last hour of the trip to Luxor is green as canals irrigate the desert the closer we get to Nile River where sugar cane and bananas are harvested.

Luxor, Egypt

The walk along the Avenue of Sphinxes on the way to the Temple of Luxor on the banks of the Nile River is absolutely breathtaking. From childhood National Geographic photos of this world famous site have always fascinated me and to finally be a part of it taking my own photos is exhilarating.

It only gets better as we approach the Temple of Luxor with two gigantic statues of Ramses and one of the two obelisks adorning the entrance. Mohammed Ali who ruled Egypt in the early 19th Century gave the other obelisk to France as a gift that today is the centerpiece of Place de la Concorde in Paris. The temple was completed by the 18th Dynasty Pharaoh Amenhotep III and added to by Ramses II during the next dynasty.

Thebes, Egypt

A visit to the Valley of the Kings (1500 BC) and the 62 tombs is a remarkable experience. All but three tombs have been raided and their treasures stolen leaving the Tomb of Tutankhamun, the last tomb to be discovered in 1922 with King Tut's vast treasures completely in tact. A few tombs are wheel chair accessible but some are not. King Tut's tomb is not, but the treasures have been removed and are on display in the Egyptian Museum in Cairo on the second floor. Hopefully, wheel chair access may become available to this second floor in the near future.

Similarly, the Valley of the Queens nearby contains nearly 80 tombs of royal wives and children with the most famous the Tomb of Queen Nefertari considered by some as the most beautiful tomb in Egypt.

On our return from the West bank from the Nile River we stopped to see the Queen Hatshepsut Temple, a magnificent architectural structure blending in with the environment designed by Senenmut in the 18 dynasty.

Before crossing the Nile again to the east bank we stopped to photograph the Colossi of Memnon that are two 60-foot high statues of Amenhotep III.

Suez Canal, Egypt.

Debbie and I traversed the Panama Canal on the Cunard Sagafjord in 1993 so this was to be our first trip through the Suez Canal. The two canals are quite different from each other. The Panama Canal through a series of locks lifts a ship up from one ocean to a lake that a ship crosses and thorough another series of locks sends the ship down to another ocean saving a trip around South America. The scenery on both sides of the canal is lush jungle,

Although the Suez Canal has no locks it is water filled trench across the desert from the Mediterranean Sea to the Red Sea that leads to the Indian Ocean saving a trip around Africa. The scenery on both sides of the canal is predominately desert and sand dunes with a few towns interspersed. Ships going the opposite direction in the Suez Canal sometimes appear as a mirage of a ship moving in sand as the dunes prevent you from seeing they are in the water.

Both canals are equally interesting and many on board ship stayed out on deck all day to view the unusual scenery and passing ships. The French completed the Suez Canal in 1869 and today it belongs to Egypt.

Port Said, Egypt

One of two seaports for visiting Cairo and the Pyramids. The other is Alexandria about the same distance from Cairo and each port is at least three hours from Cairo. Port Said has many wealthy homes on the Mediterranean and is a Mecca for vacationing

Memphis, Egypt.

Only 12 miles from Cairo, Memphis was founded in 3100 BC and was Egypt's ancient capital. Memphis ranks as the oldest city we have visited to date, 5800 years old. We were able to see the statue of Ramses II who ruled Egypt from 1290 to 1294 BC among the many artifacts of early Memphis.

Sakkara, Egypt

Site of the Step Pyramid of Djoser is the oldest of all the pyramids in Egypt and in fact is the oldest structure in the world built in 2700 BC. The architect Imhotep whose name means "He comes in peace" designed the step pyramid for the pharaoh.

Each step of pyramid is ten meters high. Close observation of the pyramid one can see the correction made to the left corner of the first step. Part way through construction the Pharaoh decided he would like a height of 60 meters, so Imhotep extended the left side of the base to allow the increase in height to six steps.

Debbie was inspired by this sight and I balanced her standing without holding on to anything and cautiously backed away from her to take her picture standing alone in the desert before the Step Pyramid of Djoser, Today she loves this photo and regrets she did not remove her sunglasses.

Giza, Egypt

The Pyramids of Giza remain the lone survivor of the Ancient Seven Wonders of the World. They were constructed from 2686-2181 BC and are absolutely breathtaking as you stand before them. The three main Pyramids and satellite pyramids are dominated by the Great Pyramid built for the 4th Dynasty King Khufu and remained for centuries as the tallest building in the world until the more recent 19th century. Guarding the entrance to the Giza plateau is the Sphinx a statue of a man on the body of perhaps a lion considered by many the earliest known monumental statue with estimated dating of 2500 BC.

A visit to the Giza Plateau and that only remaining Ancient Wonder of the World is awesome to say the least.

Port Said, Egypt.

It is time so say goodbye to friends made on this 35 day voyage. The ship, Oceana Nautica leaves the Suez Canal at Port Said and heads out across the Mediterranean bound for Athens. Debbie often tries to use her wheelchair as a walker early in the mornings for coffee in the lounge. By now everyone is used to seeing Debbie folding up her wheelchair and trying to walk the 20 feet to the window holding on to furniture where she sits every morning. Chester Stone, William Studd, James Ethan Allen and Jerry Blaine were usually there to help her if I were not.

When a trip like this comes to an end, after meeting such wonderful travel companions, there is a certain sadness that prevails after 35 days of great times.

Ancient Wonder of the World, The Pyramid at Giza

Temple of Amun, Karnak, Egypt

Patrol on Camel Saffaga, Egypt

Last remaining Ancient Wonder of the World, Pyramids of Giza

The Sphinx, Egypt

Welcome on our return from Cairo to Oceana Nautica

World's oldest building, Step Pyramid of Djoser, Saffaga, Egypt

CHAPTER XXVI

EUROPE, 2007

Athens, Greece

Our ship, Oceana, Nautica docked at Piraeus, Greece as it did last year and our Round the World Voyage is now complete. Last year we crossed the Atlantic Ocean to Athens and this year the Pacific Ocean to Athens having previously sailed from Los Angeles to Ft. Lauderdale, FL through the Panama Canal we gained a new experience this year in our transit through the Suez Canal.

Once again we call Cosmos one of our favorite taxi drivers, who was thrilled to hear from us again after our good times in Athens last year. He met us the ship and took us to Delphi, Greece about 3 hours North of Athens.

Delphi, Greece.

At one time about 540 BC, the holiest place in all of Greece. French archeologists expropriated the area and demolished the buildings covering many antiquities. The remains of the Temple of Apollo are now easy to see, as is the Treasury, a small Doric Temple that was reconstructed using blocks of marble from the site. The site of Delphi looks over a valley that drops over 2000 feet.

Cosmos our driver is very proud of this place. We took him to lunch on a terrace hanging over the cliff with spectacular views of the olive groves and vineyards in the valley far below.

Brussels, Belgium.

Sometimes the best bargain in airfare is not the way to travel. Our reservations from Athens to Brussels were made on Brussels Air, which allows minimal luggage. Our excess luggage charge was $457.00 US dollars. So watch out for bargain airlines that anticipate minimal luggage and avoid the surprise luggage charge..

The possibility of a scam exists at Car Rental agencies at Brussels Airport. To make sure this does not happen to you, I shall relate the incident. The cost for the mini-van seemed reasonable under $400.00 US for 7 days. The agent informed me that I must check out the car myself in the parking garage and if anything was wrong to report any damage back to him right away.

I read the car rental documents after the agent told me he sought authorization for 800.00 Euros equivalent to $1,200.00 on my credit card. I signed off on his authorization for 800 Euros. He gave me the car keys and a very large plastic folder containing the car rental documents.

The agent then informed me that car is located in the airport garage after taking an elevator down one flight. While on the elevator with a luggage cart piled high and the rental documents too large to be in ones pocket were placed on top of the luggage, three men in business suits one of them walking backwards enter the elevator and the backwards man knocks the luggage of the cart.

Profusely apologizing the three men restack the luggage and I leave the elevator toward the obscure very distant car rental car near the furthest point in the garage.

Upon loading the luggage I find I have only the car key and not the rental documents, so I return to the agent and ask him for a copy of my travel documents.

The agent refuses to give me a copy of my travel documents and informs me that there was a notice on the cover of the folder containing the travel documents stating that if lost there is a 125 Euro charge to replace the registration portion which I am told was inside the folder rather than inside the car. As the 125 Euros are equivalent to about 137.50 US dollars, it appears certainly enough profit to operate a scam a dozen or more times per day as people enter the elevator with a luggage cart. (Example $137.50 times 12 = $1614.00 per day)

Given that the registration is lost, I asked the agent to cancel the car rental and issue me another car with a current registration.

He refused to do so.

He stated that if the police stopped me, just call the agency and they would verify that the car was indeed a rental by me. I asked for at least a copy of the rental agreement I signed. He refused to accommodate me.

I escorted Debbie to the car and proceeded to Bruges without any documentation verifying that I rented this car. On the way to Bruges we discussed the situation and concluded there was a possibility that I was set up as an easy target for a scam with so much luggage.

We further concluded that the agent by requesting a credit card authorization for 800.00 Euros fully expected to charge against what could amount to 1,040.00 US dollars. It doesn't take a rocket scientist to determine the outcome, so we decided to forget returning the car to Brussels and use the excess funds to drive to drive the car all the way to Nice, France and return it to the Car Rental agency at Nice, Airport on the contracted day before the expected time. Debbie and I were not about to allow this incident to affect our positive attitude and continued to enjoy our road trip.

Worth mentioning here is that I did dispute the charges made to my credit card of $1846.73 for the mini-van and the bank credited my card $1,480.63. So in this case we snatched victory right out of the very jaws of defeat using a mini-van for a full week in Europe for $366.10. Actually the dispute sent to the bank was the eleven paragraphs above written the same evening in Bruges, Belgium.

Bruges, Belgium

We checked into the Pennenhuis Hotel in Bruges, Belgium. This hotel has wheelchair accessible rooms overlooking the garden for disabled persons, and to avoid the steps leading into the hotel we ordered our dinner as room service allowing me to document my car rental dispute on the same day.

Amsterdam, Netherlands

Lots of canals and many have told us not to miss the canal boat tours. It was in Amsterdam that we had our first rainy day so we enjoyed a wonderful steak dinner across the street from the Opera House to wait for the rain to let up. No luck at all, the rain continued and parking is a problem in Amsterdam, so we decided as long as the weather was bad to put some miles on the car heading toward Luxembourg.

Luxembourg

The Grand Hotel Cravat overlooking the town square became our home base in Luxembourg. The view from our hotel room was awesome, so good we did room service for dinner.

Leaving Luxembourg we headed for the Mosel Valley in Germany, noted for its wine and followed the Mosel River until it empties into the Rhine River at Koblentz.

Rhine River Cruise, Germany

Our objective here was to see the many castles in what Rick Steves refers to as the best part of the Rhine River. Taking his advice we took a Rhine River Cruise from St. Goar to Bacharach and return to St. Goar. Lots of different castles to view, some were used to collect tolls from passing merchants on the river in years past. Others from feudal times were barons of tiny kingdoms that later became part of a unified Germany.

The particular cruise line we used was definitely wheel chair accessible, with attendants helping the disabled on board. We had lunch in the dinning room on board and enjoyed the many sights on the Rhine.

We did drive along the Rhine River from Koblentz to Frankfort and agree that the best of the Rhine Castles is from St. Goar to Bachrach.

Romantic Road, Germany

The highlight of the Romantic Road is Rothenberg, Germany. Rothenburg is a medieval walled city with many tourist attractions. Although there are cobblestone streets, there are also sidewalks that are easy to negotiate with a wheelchair. Climbing the wall however is not wheelchair accessible but the rest of the city is definitely worth a visit.

Munich, Germany.

Last year we got lost in Munich trying to visit Nymphenburg Palace and finally gave up and left the city. I have written a book titled, *Triumph of the Swan* that could use very important supporting photos from Nymphemburg Palace especially the painting showing King Ludwig II taking his midnight sleigh ride.

It was in Nuremberg that we met a local resident in an outdoor café sitting next to us as we were having lunch. I explained how we got lost last year trying to find Nymphburg Palace. He explained that he can give me exact directions as he visits Munich often on business and can advise me how best to accomplish finding the place. He notices Debbie's wheelchair and suggested that we stay North of the city where there are numerous motels with easy wheelchair access. He actually drew me a map showing the exact location of the Palace.

As we approached Munich we started to see hotel and motel signs before entering the busy city. I selected and exit about 10 miles North of Munich and proceeded until we saw a sign Hotel Huber. My God, my dad was 100% Irish and my mother was Irish and part German with a maiden name of Huber, so with fate guiding us we stayed at a wonderful hotel, that we heartily recommend with wheelchair access and a great dinning room with exquisite food. Thanks Mom! I love you!

The young lady at the hotel desk also proved to be very helpful; she gave me her personal guide to Munich and asked that I give it back after my trip to Nymphenburg. She outlined on a map go to where the highway ends and take a right to Nymphenburg Palace.

The directions sound too easy, so I tried it and I was there.

Nymphenburg is unmistakable as I drove by it having to make a U turn to enter. I was stunned by the sheer sight of such an enormous

Palace, certainly comparable to Versailles and the Austrian Palaces of the time.

Of special interest to me in Nymphenburg Palace are artifacts of King Ludwig II who was born in this Palace. One of the buildings on the palace grounds is a museum and contains the painting that I was searching for. To may surprise, not only is the painting on display here, but so are the various sleighs and carriages used by the various Bavarian Kings.

Many historians refer to King Ludwig II as Mad King Ludwig citing his lavish spending on castles, eccentric behavior such as midnight sleigh rides, fireworks displays and financial support for Richard Wagner's operas.

With photos now in hand taken at Nymphenburg I can now go on record in disagreement with those who refer to the Bavarian King as Mad King Ludwig. It is clearly a bad rap to a very kind man as will be pointed out in my book *Triumph of the Swan*.

Debbie and I have visited all the castles built by King Ludwig II and now it is clear at Nymphenburg that Ludwig II's predecessors were very comfortable with their fancy sleighs, carriages, castles, hunting parties, house guests and eccentric behavior all of which are the privilege of Kings.

Liechtenstein

From Munich we headed south toward our destination to return the car in Nice. As we leave Germany and enter Austria we choose the direction of Liechtenstein where we have never before visited as our place to stay overnight.

Our hotel is in a valley surrounded by snow capped Alps was nice and the owner was very hospitable. He gave us maps and suggested we go Vaduz, the capital of Liechtenstein for dinner. We enjoyed a beautiful ride through the small villages until we arrived at Vaduz. The restaurant we chose had a view of the castle of the Prince of Liechtenstein.

Switzerland.

I had been to Switzerland before and stayed at Jungfrau and visited the Ice Palace high atop the Alps. This time it was leaving Liechtenstein and crossing Switzerland from North to South while heading for Italy.

The Swiss scenery is delightful; around each bend in the road is another breathtaking vista of the small villages in the Alps. After many tunnels through the mountains we finally entered the San Bernardino Tunnel that is quite long and was a marvel of construction when built.

Como, Italy.

Lake Como, Italy is one of the most scenic places we have ever been. We stayed at the Grand Palace Hotel in Como in an elegant room with a spectacular view of Lake Como.

Walking around the city of Como is truly a pleasure. There is a promenade on the Lake Front that enters parks where the locals mix with tourists to sit in park benches and just people watch as pedestrians walk by.

Como is a focal point for boating activity. Travelers can take a tour boat to explore Lake Como and the many small Italian Villages on this beautiful lake.

Ballagio, Italy

Visiting Ballagio by boat from Como is an absolute delight. The boats are reasonable in price and are wheelchair friendly. There is a dinning room on board for complete meals and a bar service with sandwiches as well. The boat left from Como and stopped at tiny Lake Como Villages all the way to Ballagio like Tavernola, Cernobbio, Multrasio, Torno, Urio, Brienno, Argegno and other quaint villages. Many villas line the shores of Lake Como in these small villages.

As the boat approached Bellagio almost everyone was outside on deck taking pictures of this scenic village. There are lots of hotels overlooking the lake, many restaurants and souvenir shops, promenades and beaches as well. The back streets of Bellagio have many steps as the town is built on a hillside with no provision for wheelchairs. However, the waterfront of Bellagio is wheelchair friendly and certainly worth a visit.

The return trip to Como was equally pleasant and Lake Como is definitely a place I would like to visit again.

Nice, France.

Last year we spent 12 days in Nice, this year we have reservations for 9 days in the same hotel, in fact the same room with a balcony overlooking the Mediterranean.

We made it from lake Como, Italy to Nice, France in three hours and the staff of the Hotel welcomed us. I returned the car at Nice, Airport by 1:00 pm thankful that we were was able to complete this seven-day auto tour from Brussels to Nice without further incident.

Cannes, France

The Cannes Film Festival was taking place during our stay in Nice that made it possible to attend this gala event from our home base in Nice. My book *Mt. Soledad Love Story* was adapted from the screenplay of the same title and I have not given up trying to have it made into a movie so attendance at a film festival is helpful.

Cosmos our cab driver takes us to Delphi, Greece

Lots of castles along the Rhine River, Germany

Bateaux-Mouche, Saine River Cruise, Paris , France

Eiffel Tower from Bateaux-Mouche, Paris, France

Lake Como, from Grand Place Hotel window

Bellagio, Italy

Balcony in Nice, France

CHAPTER XXVII

MONACO TO ENGLAND
HOLLAND AMERICA M/V
ROTTERDAM 6

Monte Carlo, Monaco

Last year we enjoyed the Casino de Monte Carlo, this year we visit Monte Carlo to embark on the Holland America Line ship RotterdamVI for a cruise to Marseille, Barcelona, Cadiz, Paris and London. To our surprise, the ship was at anchor rather than docked. The staff of Holland America lifted Debbie in her wheelchair and gently placed her in the tender, another group did the same boarding the ship from the tender. Kudos to Holland America for their attention to the disabled.

Barcelona, Spain

An unusual opportunity awaited us in Barcelona as two of Holland America's ships the Rotterdam VI that we are currently sailing and the Princendam that we have previously booked for January 2008 are docked on the same pier.

We are scheduled to circumnavigate South America and visit Antarctica on the Princendam and have been following the progress of this ship since 1993 when Berlitz gave both the Cunard Sagafjord and Cunard Royal Viking Sun, (now the Princendam) its highest rating, so curiosity got the best of us and we spent the morning exploring this beautiful ship.

The Princendam lived up to our expectations, a small ship by today's standards designed for 793 passengers, beautifully appointed, and wonderful cuisine. We had lunch on board and marveled over our good choice for our January 2008 cruise.

Leaving the Princendam we entered Barcelona from the waterfront and took photos of the massive column with a statue of Christopher Columbus at the top. We walked the length of Las Ramblas one of Europe's most famous promenades. Yes, Las Ramblas is wheelchair friendly even to the extreme, not even a bump between the Columbus Column and the Placa de Cataluna.

Walking the entire length of Las Ramblas we did get plenty thirsty and took note of the many outdoor cafes lining the promenade and selected a Tapas Café to stop at on our way back. Passing lots of shops and booths along the promenade we bought some souvenirs and headed back to quench our thirst. We stopped at Tapa Apat and ordered two giant beers, so big that Debbie could hardly lift hers.

The Tapa Apat outdoor café is quite nice, serving tapas in the center of tables on a multi-layered lazy-Suzan. We already had lunch on the Princendam but Debbie spotted the irresistible Mussels Marianne, and had a second lunch to accompany her giant beer.

Barcelona has so much art and architecture that it would not be possible to take it all in on a one day port of call. The Gothic Quarter, the Sagrada Famila, Picasso Museum, and Joan Miro's Art will all have to wait for another trip, as we became so content just people watching with a cold beer on Las Ramblas.

Cadiz, Spain

The Phoenicians started this city about 1000 BC and it changed hands so many times, by the Carthaginians who took the city in 501 BC, then the Romans in 201 BC. The Visigoths destroyed the city in 500 AD and the Moors rebuilt it in 711 and the King of Castile and Leon eventually took it in 1262.

Cadiz became a wealthy city after the time of Columbus as a busy port trading with the Americas. Sir Frances Drake raided the port twice and the English later plundered the city, followed by the French and finally during the Spanish Civil War, Cadiz returned to Spain.

Cadiz is one of Europe's oldest cities and contains a beautiful cathedral and some Moorish Architecture as well as the remains of the Roman Theatre. All are photo opportunities and a wheelchair can go up to the edge of the Roman Theatre dating from 60AD and peer into it as if from the last row.

You can push a wheelchair for miles in Cadiz, especially in the Old City and not encounter a curb. The city has done a wonderful job of preserving its architecture and art and is today noted for its beautiful beaches attracting visitors from all parts of Europe.

Lisbon, Portugal.

On our visit last year we did not see much of Lisbon because we traveled through it on the way to Fatima. This year however, we went to the city square and walked along Rue Augusta that is like a pedestrian Mall with many shops.

No real attempt has been made to make this street wheelchair friendly and just a minimal attempt is all that is required as the curbs are sometimes only three inches high. Pushing a wheelchair requires negotiating these ancient marble curbs, but the trip is still worth the effort to see the center of Lisbon.

Paris, France

I had previously spent a week in Paris and last year Debbie and I went into Paris by train from Blois in the Chateau Region. This year however our ship docked at La Harve a full three hours from Paris. Our plan was to take a cab from the ship to the train station and travel by train to Paris. Our cab driver Olivier was so gracious that we decided to hire him for the day and forget the train, as we were to have more flexibility by cab.

"Where would you like to go?" Olivia inquired.

"The Bateaux-Mouches is my number one priority this year. Each year I intend to take this Seine River Cruise and it never gets done and this year I think Debbie will enjoy it."

"Debbie, you will certainly enjoy the Bateaux-Mouches," offers Olivia. In fact, you will have easy access with a wheelchair from the parking area at Pont de l'Alma where I can drive right up to the boat".

"Sounds good", says Debbie.

"How about a stop at Versaille on the way into Paris so Debbie can see the Palace?"

"Sure, it is on the way, the grounds and gardens are equally beautiful, I used to take my wife there for walks often."

Olivia pointed out the Petite Trinon and the Hameau, favorite retreats of Marie-Antoinette where she could drop out and tend her private garden.

The Gardens at Versaille are exquisite and often used as a standard by European Royalty in the construction of their own palaces.

From the Gardens of Versaille we headed for Paris where Olivia pulled his cab up right next to the Bateau-Mouches.

I bought Olivia a ticket to go with us, and he was thrilled.

Getting Debbie on board in a wheelchair was no problem and we put her next to a window where she couldn't miss the sights. The Bateaux –Mouche left the dock and we were on our way on our first Seine River Cruise.

What a wonderful relaxing way to see Paris. Last year I pushed the wheelchair from the Arch de Triumph to Place de Concorde. Bateaux-Mouches is the way to go, you glide past the Cathedral de Notre Dame, Musee D'Orsay, the Louvre, Place de Concorde, and so many wonderful examples of Parisian architecture.

The Batuaux is very low to fit under all the bridges and each time we go under a bridge, the school-children in the back of the boat clap and cheer, which eventually makes you laugh.

"So Debbie, are you having fun yet?" I ask.

"Fantastic", she says, "perfect for the disabled."

As we pull up to the dock, Olivia asks, "What next?"

La Pied de Cauchon for lunch if it is still there!

"Great choice!"   "Yes it is still there, and is a favorite of Parisians."

"In 1975 when I was there last they had a small pig tied to a fire hydrant near the front door and their specialty was pigs feet." "Thus their name in English is translated, *at the foot of the pig.*"

La Pied du Cuchon is near the Paris Opera and it is difficult to park, so Olivia dropped us off at the front door.

"Olivia, we are buying you lunch, so you have to get rid of this cab and we will wait for you at a front table."

Minutes later, Olivia shows up with a big smile and tells the waiter I was here 32 years ago.

"Where is the pig tied to the fire hydrant?" I ask.

"Someone must have ate it', offers Olivia.

We had a wonderful lunch in this beautiful French Restaurant.

On the 3 hour drive back to Le Harve on the seacoast we were able to reminisce on how perfect the day was.

As we pulled up to the ship, Olivia gave Debbie an Eiffel Tower Key Chain to remember this eventful day.

Harwich, England

Our cruise on the Rotterdam VI ended at Harwich that is a seaport about two hours North of London. The ship provided us with transfers to Heathrow Airport for our 55 minute flight to Cork Ireland.

B&B in Cork , Ireland

Produce Market, Hobart, Tasmania, Australia

Blarney Caastle, Blarney, Ireland

Great Barrier Reef Hotel, Cairns, Australia

Our balcony, Nice, France

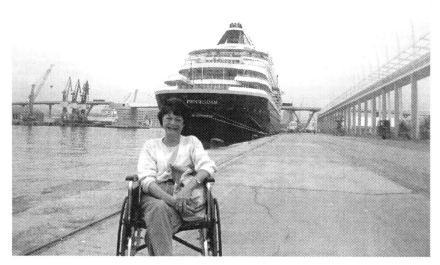

Lunch aboard the Princendam, Barcelona, Spain

CHAPTER XVIII

IRELAND

My ancestors came from Ireland during the great immigration to America. My father's sister Marian Roach claims that seven Roche Brothers left Cork Ireland for America and when they arrived at Ellis Island their name was Americanized from Roche to Roach.

As much as Debbie and I dislike flying we flew from London to Cork, Ireland in 55 minutes on Aer Lingus rather than cross the Irish Sea by boat which takes nearly a day.

A National Car Rental was reserved for us at Cork Airport and within a few minutes of landing we were on our way to the city without the ordeal we found in Brussels.

Our car rental is a four-door sedan to accommodate a wheelchair in the back seat, as the trunk is full of luggage. In Ireland, renting a large car can be a terrifying mistake unless you like white knuckles while you drive. With so many narrow Irish roads a small car would be a better choice.

Cork

Cork is a beautiful small city with the navigable River Lee surrounding the city center. One can visualize the masted ships of the 1800s tied to the quay waiting to take so many Irish to America. Debbie and I stayed in a B&B across the street from the University in downtown Cork. The B&B, three stories high caught my immediate attention as is identical to my grandparents home in Union City, NJ. Architecturally it is Pullman style with a hallway and stairs to the upper floors on the left. The front room has a fireplace and is typically the living room, behind that is a dining room accessed through an arch from the Front Room or from the Pullman style hallway. Behind the dining room are the kitchen and bathrooms and bedrooms, only accessed from the hallway.

So many Roach family gatherings did I enjoy with my grandparents and later my Aunt Marian Roach until she passed away in a near identical building, that the nostalgia caught up with me. It did strike me that the Roach clan came to America and had a house built that was typical of homes they left behind in Ireland.

I probably still have relatives here in Cork, but with so little time remaining I had to move on. Staying in this B&B in Cork brought tears to my eyes reminiscing on so many happy times with my grandparents, parents and aunts all of which influenced the course of my life and are now fond memories that make me smile.

Blarney

A few miles north of Cork lays the quaint little town of Blarney. We knew as soon as we entered town a great adventure awaited us. Rain was threatening so we headed for Blarney Castle. Originally the castle was built as a wooden structure in the tenth century and was replaced by stone in 1210 AD with additions made to the keep in 1446, Blarney Castle is impressive.

As we approached the castle we took a few photos and of course the inevitable rain started so I wheeled Debbie into the Dungeon at the foot of the castle to get out of the rain. It was in the dungeon that we read the may conflicting tales concerning the Blarney Stone, from the stone mentioned in the Bible as "Jacob's pillow" and brought to Ireland by either Jeremiah the Prophet or perhaps placed in Ireland during the Crusades. Another tale is at the time of Cormac McCarthy, who supposedly supplied 4000 men to Robert the Bruce at the Battle of Bannockburn received half the stone of Scone in gratitude.

Queen Elizabeth I sent the Earl of Leichester to take the castle and McCarthy wined and dined him so often to delay his losing possession. When Queen Elizabeth I read the Earls reports of him not yet taking the castle, she uttered, "Blarney!"

Legend continues that to whom the stone is kissed the gift of eloquence is bestowed.

Those of us huddled in the dungeon discussed the 125 steps to the top of castle to kiss the Blarney Stone. There is no way Debbie can climb these steps so she asked that I kiss the stone twice, once for her.

Leaving Debbie in the Dungeon, I entered the castle and started the climb. Very narrow, pie shaped stone steps limits the disabled from this exciting adventure. Various rooms of the castle lead off this circular staircase, such as the Great Hall, Family Room, Guest Rooms, Chapel and Kitchen. At the very top on the roof behind a parapet is the Blarney Stone.

Visitors are lined up waiting to kiss the stone, which involved lying on your back while an attendant holds you and leaning over backwards until your head is much lower than your body and kissing the Blarney Stone. In my case I kissed it twice, once for Debbie,

A poem attributed to Francis Sylvester Mahoney regarding the stone follows:

"There is a stone that whoever kisses,

Oh! He never misses to grow eloquent

'Tis he may clamber to a lady's chamber,

Or become a member of parliament."

Dingle

The Dingle Peninsula is a very special place. The Gallic language is quite well preserved here.

David Lean the film producer who filmed Lawrence of Arabia and Doctor Zhivago both containing spectacular scenery, chose the Dingle Peninsula for his film Ryan's daughter, starring Robert Mitchem. The film finished way over budget because of so much rain and Robert Mitchim with considerable idle time, brought a lot of worldwide attention to this beautiful part of Ireland that juts out into the sea.

Naturally fascinated by all this natural beauty and folklore we headed for Dingle. The roads, extremely narrow with many curves rattled our nerves as cars passed us in the opposite direction. We stopped for a while in Inch, a small town on the peninsula with beautiful beaches. Finally we reached Dingle the primary town of the peninsula and found a wonderful B&B right on the waters edge.

Dingle is a wheelchair friendly town so minutes after we arrived we were walking through the town searching for a Pub that served fish and chips. Not difficult tasks as there are so many Pubs, some even next door to each other. A pint of Guiness and Fish and Chips made a tasty lunch.

The locals ask where we are from and we say San Diego. They all know where that is and ask a lot of questions one of which concerns my last name Roach that in Ireland is Roche.

Walking around Dingle is a lot of fun; people are so friendly and helpful. They enjoy conversation with visitors. We explored the town, the fishing fleet at the pier and many different Pubs before returning to the B&B.

A heavy rainstorm was now pelting Dingle but we were already sheltered inside and the hostess, Eileen asked:

"What would you like for breakfast in the morning"?

"Continental or the Full Irish Breakfast?"

Debbie and I both opted for the Irish Breakfast.

The next morning, there it was, a full Irish Breakfast for two, set in their dining room overlooking the sea. Bacon, eggs, sausage, coffee, juice, toast in a rack etc. etc. The howling storm was still raging outside, so I asked Eileen:

"Will this awful rain ever let up"?

"That's not rain," she says; "it's Irish Mist!"

"Ha! I'll have to remember that one."

We left in the pouring rain and crossed the Dingle Peninsula to the Northeast and as we approached Tralee the rain let up and the sun came out allowing us to enjoy the sight of so many farms, each marked with stone boundaries and some with sheep grazing on the plush green hillsides.

Dublin

Heading for Dublin from Limerick early in the morning was an easy 2-hour ride, mostly on divided highways with wide shoulders. Halfway to Dublin the rain started up again with gale force winds so the windshield wipers were working at top speed trying to keep up.

"Just a little Irish Mist," I said to Debbie, and we both laughed.

"I think we should forget the Guiness Factory Tour and downtown Pubs with all this rain," she offered.

"I agree. "At this point I will be happy to check in to the hotel and return this car, so we make our flight to London in the morning without delay."

"What did you think of Ireland, Debbie?"

"I loved it, the people are charming, the scenery is spectacular and everything is so green. I saw enough to make me want to come back again, even with a little less Irish Mist."

"Ha!" was my response.

English Pub aboard the Queen Mary 2

Big Beers, Barcelona, Spain

Her second lunch, Las Ramblaas, Barcelona, Spain

Lisbon, Portugal

CHAPTER XXIX

TRANSLANTIC CROSSING
SOUTHAMPTON, ENGLAND
TO NEW YORK
CUNARD, QUEEN MARY 2

ENGLAND.

London, England

We saw about two hours of the English countryside by traveling from the port of Harwich, north of London's Heathrow airport for our flight to Ireland. Again on returning from Dublin to London we traveled an additional two hours south to the port of Southampton, England. We were so intent on visiting Ireland that we put off visiting London until perhaps, next year.

Southampton, England

It is here at the Southern tip of England that we board the Ocean Liner, Queen Mary 2 for a transatlantic crossing to New York. The Queen

Mary 2 is a beautiful ship and makes the Atlantic Crossing in six days in complete luxury.

New York, NY

The Statue of Liberty greets us two years in a row in New York Harbor and as usual we regret this wonderful trip now coming to an end. Our Round the World Cruise was actually completed in Athens as in 2006 we crossed the Atlantic to Athens and this year 2007 we crossed the Pacific Ocean to Athens. The obvious questions are why not fly home from Athens, rather than cross the Atlantic last year on M/S Amsterdam and this year on the Queen Mary 2.

Airline regulation imposing multiple hardships on its passengers is certainly helping the Cruise Line Industry. With baby-boomers reaching retirement age, they will have the time to cruise instead of fly. Any flight over five hours is too much for Debbie, so crossing the Atlantic on a ship in 6 relaxing, luxurious days is our obvious choice.

We still have to fly home to San Diego from New York City and we know beforehand how we might as well call it a lost day in our lives. Get to the airport 2 hours before the flight, submit to the latest regulations, board the plane for a 5 hour flight in not very comfortable seats, add to this that a two-hour delay sitting on the runway in line waiting to take off then land at San Diego and wait at the carousel up to and ½ hour for your luggage, then search for your missing luggage and fill out missing luggage forms and get a taxi cab home. Between nine hours and eleven hours wasted depending on how long it took to get clearance for take off in New York, so call it a day shot.

Fortunately we have another cruise to look forward to on January 3, 2008

CHAPTER XXX

WHAT NEXT?
ANTARCTICA AND SOUTH AMERICA,
HOLLAND AMERICA, M/V
PRINCENDAM

We booked this cruise in January 2007 even before we left for the first leg of our 2007 Round the World Cruise on the QE 2. The ship M/V Princendam is a small and intimate ship that requires an early booking and leaves Ft. Lauderdale on Jan 3, 2008.

We prey our health holds up so we can complete this cruise as a visit to Antarctica will complete our visit to the 7 continents.

We have cruised through the Panama Canal in 1993, so the Princendam Cruise in 2008 will be our second transit. Once through the canal from the Atlantic to the Pacific the Princendam visits Ecuador and Peru, and hopefully a visit to Machu Pichu, (not for Debbie, I am sure) and maybe not for me if breathing is difficult at that altitude. From Peru we visit many ports in Chile and cruise the Straights of Magellan with a port of call at Ushuaia, Argentina, before rounding Cape Horn and heading to Antarctica. It can then be recorded in my own travel diary that I have visited Point Barrow, Alaska, the northernmost town in North America, as well as Ushuaia, Argentina, the southernmost town in South America.

The Princendam then cruises a few days in Antarctica to see up close the sights of Antarctica before heading for South Georgia and the Falkland Islands where we can mingle with the Penguins.

Other highlights of this cruise include two days in Buenos Aires, Argentina, a day in Montevideo, Uruguay, two days in Rio de Janeiro, Brazil and cruising the Amazon River all the way to Manaus, Brazil where we again enjoy another two days.

There are many other ports of call not mentioned as this chapter attempts only to show the direction of the Circumnavigation of South America. There is no reason to hold up the printing of this book when so many disabled people could benefit from its contents now.

The next chapter discusses our 1993 Panama Canal Cruise in detail to give the reader an idea of why we look forward to our second transit through the canal in January 2008..

Panama Canal

Copacabana Beach in distance

Churrascarias at Marius

Christ the Redeemer, Rio de Janeiro, Brazil

CHAPTER XXXI

CUNARD, HMS SAGAFJORD 1993 PANAMA CANAL AND BRAZIL CRUISE

The book was sent to the publisher in September of 2007 and we look forward to continued good health to once again transit the canal together on our way to Antarctica on January 3, 2008. The Panama Canal and Rio de Janeiro certainly should be included as highlights in any round the world adventure, so included here are highlights form our travel diary that we hope to experience again.

PANAMA CANAL.

We awoke and went out on deck to see lots of ships waiting their turn to enter the Panama Canal. As our turn came the Sagafjord lifted anchor and proceeded under the Pan American Highway Bridge to enter the first lock. Debbie and I spent the entire day on deck, as did most passengers who did not want to miss anything. The ship is towed through the locks by a machine on a railroad track called a mule. The third lock from the Pacific Ocean lifted us up 85 feet to enter Miraflos and Gatun Lakes, both beautiful with dense jungle right up to the shoreline.

In a narrow lake passage we saw the plaque on shore memorializing the 25,000 lives lost in the construction of the canal. By sunset we had descended through three locks to the Gatun Lock which opened and released the Sagafjord to sail the Atlantic Ocean

From Balboa, Panama on the Pacific to Cristobal, Panama on the Atlantic is a fascinating experience, and a perfect first cruise for a couple seeking adventure. Some actually refer to the Panama Canal as the Eighth Wonder of the World. Curiously in 2007 in an Internet poll for new wonders of the world, the Panama Canal was not even mentioned. Debbie and I look forward to another trip through this magnificent canal in 2008.

BRAZIL

Our second cruise on the Sagafjord took us from Ft. Lauderdale, FL to Rio de Janeiro Brazil with ports of call at Barbados, French Guiana's Devils Island, and the Brazilian ports of Fortaleza, Recife, Vitoria and Rio de Janeiro. My luggage did not arrive from my flight until we got to Barbados and if it were not for the kindness of the H. Stern salesmen on board that lent me dinner jackets etc, it could have been a problem. They also taught me a few Portuguese words and invited us to their showrooms when we arrive in Rio.

Rio de Janeiro

Debbie and I awoke early so that we could see the ship enter the harbor of Rio. I do not expect to see many sights in the world to be more beautiful than this one. Sugarloaf Mountain is on our left and Corcavado on our right with the statue of Christ the Redeemer high atop the mountain with arms outstretched welcoming ships into the harbor.

Our Sagafjord cruise ended in Rio de Janeiro and we had hotel reservations at the Sheraton Rio for a few days to explore this beautiful city. The Jewelers at H. Sterns in Rio had a limo waiting to take us to the Sheraton Rio gratis that we accepted. H. Sterns has a jewelry store inside the Sheraton Rio, where I bought Debbie a rainbow tennis bracelet adorned with the jewels of Brazil.

Rio has so much to offer that we were happy we decided to stay a few extra days. We hired Oscar Meco a cab driver for our entire stay. The Sheraton Rio is a few miles south of Ipemena. We chose this hotel for its security and private beach.

The first day in Rio, Oscar took us to Sugarloaf Mountain where be boarded a two stage cable car that took us 1293 feet above the harbor. While we were admiring this spectacular view we heard some noise over the cliff. We looked over the edge and saw two mountain climbers with spikes and ropes climbing the face of Sugarloaf and just reaching the crest right below at our feet. They reached the pinnacle and stood up coiled their ropes and walked off as if this was a routine occurrence.

The next morning Oscar took us to the hippie fair at Ipamena that is an outdoor market held only on Sundays with hundreds of booths with all kinds of Brazilian trinkets. From the hippie fair we went to Cococabana Palace Hotel and invited Oscar to join us. We later sat in sidewalk cafes at Cococabana Beach admiring the bikinis and mosaic sidewalks over a cool beer.

That same afternoon it was time to go to the top of Corcovado to see for ourselves up close the statue of Christ the Redeemer. This statue is awesome and inspirational. I only wish the minority of people trying to topple the cross atop Mt. Soledad in La Jolla California could visit this place and see for themselves how this mountain top statue became the National Symbol of Brazil. My book, Mt. Soledad Love Story, shows the futility of minorities wishing to topple the cross atop Mt. Soledad.

Dinner at Marius Churrascarias was a Brazilian treat with strips of beef, sausage, chicken, lamb chops, steak served gaucho style on a sword right off the charcoal fire. Marius Churrascarias is considered one of Rio's finest restaurants and to us it lived up to its reputation.

The next evening we tried another great restaurant Mediterraneo that specializes in Seafood. We had a wonderful dinner with a good seat by an open window overlooking Ipemena. On our return to Rio we would certainly like to visit again these two restaurants. Following dinner we went to the Brazilian Show called Platforma I. This show features spectacular Brazilian dancing with beautiful scantly clad women with feather hats and lots of jewelry and makeup.

Debbie said, you wouldn't dare?

Before you new it I was up on stage dancing the samba with these gals all of which appeared a foot taller than me with all those fancy feathers and big hats adorned with leaves, flowers and bananas.

The next morning back at the hotel people asked, "Was that you I saw dancing with all those women on stage last night at the Platforma I Show?

With only one day left in Rio, we just wanted to relax, Oscar took us to the Botanical Gardens where we walked around and enjoyed such a quiet beautiful place. We took Oscar out to lunch again at Copacabana Beach where he made us promise that when we come back to Rio that we use his cab. Oscar admired my San Diego Padres baseball cap so at the airport it became his.

In our travels we often think of Louis Armstrong's inspiring song,

"What a Wonderful World"!

THE END

BIBLIOGRAPHY

Bateaux-Mouches, Dupuis 1949.   Tout Paris sur Seine, Plan de Parcours, 2007 Paris, France.

Blarney Castle, A Souvenir Guide Book, Blarney Castle Co, Cork, Ireland Publisher, John Hinde, Ltd. Dublin, Ireland
Cunard Daily Program, Historic Day for Cunard, Feb.20, 2007, Cunard Daily Program, Queen Elizabeth 2, Silver Jubilee World Cruise.
DK Eyewitness Travel Guides, Australia, Duncan Baird Publishers, London, England 2002.
Heyerdahl, Thor, *Kon Tiki, Across the Pacific by Raft,* 1950, Rand McNally Company, Chicago.
Nice-Matin, Festival du Cannes, 16 Mai 2007, Le Guide to 60e Festivval, p. 37 – 40. Nice, France.
Pan Am. *Pan Am's World Guide, Encyclopedia of Travel.* McGraw Hill Company, New York, NY.
Severin, Tim. *The Brendan Voyage: A leather boat tracks the discovery of America by the Irish Saints,* McGraw Hill Publishing Company, 1978
Steves, Rick, *The Best Of Europe, Make the Most of Every Day and Every Dollar.* 1995, John Muir Publications, Santa Fe, NM.
Stone, Irving, *The Greek Treasure,* A Biographical Novel of Henry and Sophia Schliemann, 1975
Sydney, Daily Telegraph, Her Majesties In Sydney, pages 32, 41, 3 and cover page, Feb. 21, 2007, Sydney Australia.
Sydney, Sunday Morning Herald, *Ships in the night, they dwarfed the harbor.* Feb.21, 2007 Sydney, Australia.
Ward, Douglas, *Berlitz Complete Guide to Cruising and Cruise Ships,* 1995, Berlitz Publishing Company, New York, NY
Wills, Elspeth, *The Fleet, 1840-2004, Cunard's Flagships and floating palaces from the earliest days of steam to Queen Mary 2.* 2004, The Open Agency Limited, London.
Utzon, Jorn, *The Foreward, Building a Masterpieece: The Sydney Opera House.* Editor, Anne Wasson, Powerhouse Publishing.

THE SHIPS

CUNARD
HMS Sagafjord   Panama Canal Cruise, Los Angeles to Ft. Lauderdale, 1993
HMS Sagafjord   Brazil Cruise, Ft. Lauderdale to Rio de Janerio, Brazil. 1993

HMS Queen Mary -- Now the Hotel Queen Mary, stayed aboard, Long Beach, CA 1994
HMS Queen Elizabeth 2, Los Angeles to Sydney, Australia. 2007
HMS Oueen Mary 2 Trans Atlantic, Southampton, England to New York, 2007

CELEBRITY CRUISE LINE (formerly Chandris Cruise Line)
MV Galexy. Transatlantic, Galveston TX to Rome, Italy. 2006
MV Amerikanis, Martinique, St. Lucia, Guadelope, Barbados, St. Maartin, St. John,1990
MV Azur, Martinique, St. Vincent, St. Kitts, Tortola, St Thomas, Bequia, Puerto Rico
SS Regina, Curacoa, Jamica, Bahamas

OCEANA CRUISE LINE
M/S Nautica, Black Sea Cruise. Athens to Yalta, Odessa and Istanbul, 2006
M/S Nautica, Istanbul to Greek Islands to Venice, 2006
M/S Nautica, Venice to Barcelona, 2006
M/S Nautica, Hong Kong to Bali, Shanghai, Luxor, Cairo and Athens, 2007

HOLLAND AMERICA CRUISE LINE
MS Amsterdam, Baltic Sea Cruise. Copenhagen to St. Petersburg, Russia, 2006
MS Amsterdam, Trans Atlantic, Baltic Sea to Iceland, Greenland, New York City, 2006.
MS Statendam, Sydney Australia to Bejing and Dalian, China, 2007
MS Rotterdam VI, Monte Carlo, Monaco, to Harwich, England, 2007
MS Princendam, Circumnavigate South America, Ft. Lauderdale to Antarctica, 2008

Lightning Source UK Ltd.
Milton Keynes UK
31 January 2011

166665UK00002B/197/A

9 781434 341426